His Touch on the Mouths

His Touch on the Mouths

New Perspective on the Baptism of the Holy Spirit

Seock-Tae Sohn

WIPF & STOCK · Eugene, Oregon

HIS TOUCH ON THE MOUTHS
New Perspective on the Baptism of the Holy Spirit

Copyright © 2018 Seock-Tae Sohn. All rights reserved. Except for brief quotations in critical publications or reviews, no part of this book may be reproduced in any manner without prior written permission from the publisher. Write: Permissions, Wipf and Stock Publishers, 199 W. 8th Ave., Suite 3, Eugene, OR 97401.

Wipf & Stock
An Imprint of Wipf and Stock Publishers
199 W. 8th Ave., Suite 3
Eugene, OR 97401

www.wipfandstock.com

Biblical quotations are from the *Biblia Hebraica Stuttgartensia* (*BHS*); *Novum Testamentum Graece*, Nestle-Aland, 28th ed. (NA[28]); and English Standard Version (ESV), unless otherwise specified.

The Holy Bible, English Standard Version® (ESV®) copyright © 2001 by Crossway, a publishing ministry of Good News Publishers. All rights reserved.

PAPERBACK ISBN: 978-1-5326-5581-4
HARDCOVER ISBN: 978-1-5326-5582-1
EBOOK ISBN: 978-1-5326-5583-8

Manufactured in the U.S.A.   02/04/19

For my family:
Hee Sook, Sooyun, Hwa Chang,
Sunyong, Do Rim, Joan, Joshua, Soomin

Contents

Preface | IX

Abbreviations | XII

Introduction | XV

1. The Baptism of the Holy Spirit | 1
    The Promise of the Baptism of the Holy Spirit | 1
    The Coming of the Holy Spirit | 2

2. The Prophets: The Mouth of the Lord | 9
    The Spokesman of God | 9
    The Installation of a Prophet | 10

3. The Great Prophet | 15

4. The Great Prophet Appoints His Disciples as Prophets | 19
    The Baptism of the Holy Spirit | 21
    Peter's Understanding of the Baptism of the Holy Spirit | 23
    The Disciples Acknowledged as the New Covenant Prophets | 27
        Acknowledgement by Three Thousand People | 27
        Acknowledgement by Five Thousand with the Religious Leaders | 30

5. The Activities of the New Covenant Prophets | 32
    God's Vision of New Creation | 32

Disciples' Ministry of the Word as the New Covenant
Prophets | 38
    Peter and John at Jerusalem | 38
    Philip at Judea and Samaria | 41
    Ananias at Damascus | 43
    To the End of the Earth | 45
        Antioch | 45
        Ephesus | 46
        Rome | 48

6 The Related Themes and Their Applications | 52
    The Once-and-for-Allness of the Baptism of the Holy
        Spirit | 52
        "Johannine Pentecost" | 56
        Peter and the Household of Cornelius | 62
        Paul and the Ephesian Disciples | 66
        Three thousand People Baptized at Pentecost | 69
    The Baptism of the Holy Spirit and Regeneration | 71
    The Baptism of the Holy Spirit and the Church | 75
    The Baptism of the Holy Spirit and the Baptism of
        Water | 80
    The Baptism of the Holy Spirit and the Fullness of the Holy
        Spirit | 83
    The Gifts of the Holy Spirit | 87
        Tongues | 91
            Tongues as the Gifts | 91
            The Rules for Speaking in Tongues | 93
        Prophecy | 97
            The Meaning of Prophecy | 97
            Prophecy as the Gifts | 100
            Prophecy and Tongues | 101

Conclusion | 105

Bibliography | 107

Author Index | 113

Bibliography | 117

Preface

Most Christians believe that the fire of the Holy Spirit came down to Jesus' disciples at Pentecost. From this they draw all kinds of theologies, practical principles, and applications regarding the life and growth of a Christian. Therefore, the baptism of the Holy Spirit has occupied a central place in modern Christianity. The problem, however, is that there is no unified explanation about the baptism of the Holy Spirit and its role in the life of believers. The broad and diverse views on this issue have led many to follow their own theories. It seems no consensus been reached from the postapostolic period to this present day.

In this book, I suggested an entirely different interpretation of this event from a biblical, theological, and redemptive historical point of view along with practical answers and applications. According to my observation, there was no fire coming down at Pentecost. The divided tongues like fire came down on the disciples. It was divided tongues in the form of fire, not fire in the form of tongues. There were many tongues, not just one tongue. As the tongues came down and rested on each one of them, they were all filled with the Holy Spirit and began to speak in other languages as the Spirit gave them utterance.

In order to understand this phenomenon, I began from the Old Testament. God's restoration plan for the fallen world was to realize it through the work of the word. For this purpose, God called the prophets and appointed them by touching his hands on their mouths (Jer 1:9; Isa 6:7). Thus, the prophets were called "the

Preface

mouth of the Lord" (*pi YHWH*). God committed this ministry of the word to his prophets all through the period of the Old Testament. But later, God, the word himself, came into this world as Jesus, as the great prophet promised in Deut 18:18. The three years of Jesus' ministry was a work of the word. Together with his public ministry, he trained his disciples to be the prophets for the new covenant of new ages. The narrative of the great commission in Matt 28:16–20 is almost parallel to the call of prophets in the OT. If the disciples were to be the prophets of a new covenant after the great prophet, they needed to be appointed and be testified as the one sent by God, by the Holy Spirit. They needed the prophetic authority and power from above to do the work of the word. The event at Pentecost was the ceremony of God's sealing of Jesus' disciples for the prophets by touching their mouths with the Holy Spirit. Then the disciples spoke in different languages, which was a sign demonstrating their authority as prophets before the people. After the event of Pentecost, the book of Acts traces the activities of the new covenant prophets, the ministry of the word from Jerusalem to Rome. We can observe here that where the word was proclaimed by the disciples, the Holy Spirit worked. We can also see how the new covenant prophets could conduct the ministry of the word after their baptism of the Holy Spirit even though they were uneducated and common Galileans. Therefore, the baptism of the Holy Spirit was primarily for the disciples' prophetic ministry of the word.

As a corollary of this interpretation, the themes involved in the baptism of the Holy Spirit are required to be reexamined and reinterpreted. The related themes such as the repetition of the baptism of the Holy Spirit, regeneration, sanctification, the beginning of the church and the age of new covenant, baptism of water and baptism of the Holy Spirit, fullness of the Holy Spirit, the gifts of the Holy Spirit, etc. are primarily to be checked.

My hope is that this new perspective on the baptism of the Holy Spirit will unite the various theories and teachings that have circulated throughout the churches. Believers will have clarity on the doctrine of regeneration, the various theories of tongues, and

Preface

the burden from the second blessings. The sound observation of the text; biblical, theological, and historical interpretation of the issues; and practical applications will surely give a fresh perspective on the baptism of the Holy Spirit. Furthermore, since we were baptized by the Holy Spirit at the time of our water baptism, we will be awakened to our responsibility as new covenant prophets.

As I write this book, I am greatly indebted to many friends. I want to give thanks to my colleagues and students who have communicated on this subject and gave me helpful and useful advice. Primarily, I want to express my sincere appreciation to Tremper Longman III, Seyoon Kim, Eiwon Kim, Goowon Kim, Guang-Chae Kim, Jonathan Won, Sarah Koh, and Manu Shetty for their genuine love, friendship, and encouragement in publishing this book. I want to give thanks to Rev. Dr. Kyung-Dae Cho, founder of Reformed Graduate University (Reformed Theological Seminary), for his constant concern and support for me. Wipf and Stock Publishers has been kind to me in publishing my writings since 2001. I am so much indebted to my wife and children all through my life. I want their love and sacrifice to be remembered in this book. In particular, I give thanks to God, who has brought me up and provided all kind of good things for me to open my eyes and concentrate on biblical studies. The biblical quotations are from BHS, NA 28, and ESV, unless specified otherwise.

Seock-Tae Sohn
Reformed Graduate University
Seoul, Korea

Abbreviations

AB	Anchor Bible
BBE	The Bible in Basic English
BECNT	Baker Exegetical Commentary on the New Testament
BHS	*Biblia Hebraica Stuttgartensia*, 1983
CR	*Corpus Reformatorum: Joannis Calvini Opera Quae Supersunt Omnia*, ed. Guilielmus Baum, Edwardus Cunitz and Eduardus Reuss (Brunswick: C. A. Schwetschke et Filium, 1863-1897)
DBI	*Dictionary of Biblical imagery*
ELB6	Elber Felder, 2006
ERV	English Revised Version, 1885
ESV	English Standard Version, 2016
EvT	*Evangelische Theologie*
ICC	International Critical Commentary
ISBE	*International Standard Bible Encyclopedia*
JSNT	*Jounal for the Study of the New Testament*
JSNTSup	Journal for the Study of the New Testament: Supplement Series
JSOT	*Journal for the Study of the Old Testament*

Abbreviations

KJV	King James Version, 1611
NA28	*Novum Testamentum Graece*, Nestle-Aland, 28th ed.
NAC	New American Commentary
NET	New English Translation
NICNT	New International Commentary of New Tesatment
NICOT	New International Commentary of Old Testament
NIDOTTE	*New International Dictionary of Old Testament Theology and Exegesis*
NIGCT	New Interantional Greek Testament Commentary
NIV	New International Version, 2011
NLT	New Living Translation
NRSV	New Revised Standard Version, 1989
RSV	Revised Standard Version
TWNT	*Theologische Wörterbuch zum Neuen Testament*
TDOT	*Theological Dictionary of the Old Testament*
TEV	Today's English Version
WBC	Word Biblical Commentary
WCF	Westminster Confession of Faith
WLC	Westminster Longer Catechism
WSC	Westminster Shorter Catechism
WTJ	*Westminster Theological Journal*
WUNT	Wischenschaftliche Untersuchungen zum Neuen Testament
ZAW	*Zeitschrift für die Alttestamentliche Wissenschaft*

Introduction

Debates regarding the interpretation and significance of the baptism of the Holy Spirit continue into the twenty-first century, without diminution or resolution. Even a definition of what is meant by "the baptism of the Holy Spirit" cannot be agreed upon, and neither has its essential nature been fully expounded.

Larry Hart in his article "Spirit Baptism: A Dimensional Charismatic Perspective" explains the baptism of the Holy Spirit by quoting James Dunn's definition:

> Dunn, in his highly influential *Baptism of the Holy Spirit*, speaks for many with these kind of programmatic statements: "Pentecost is a new beginning- the inauguration of the new age, the age of Spirit- that which had not been before" (p. 44). "For Luke Pentecost is also the beginning of the new covenant for the disciples" (p.47). "Pentecost inaugurates the age of church" (p.49). "[As a new epoch in salvation history], Pentecost can never be repeated" (53). "But in another sense [becoming a Christian] Pentecost, or rather the experience of Pentecost, can and must be repeated." (53). The Baptism in the Spirit, as always, is primarily initiatory, and only secondarily an empowering" (54).[1]

However, the problem is that it is not easy to accept the explanations of Dunn and Hart. The theological terms referred to here, such as regeneration, indwelling and fullness of the Spirit, covenant,

---

1. Hart, "Spirit Baptism," 117.

Introduction

union with Christ, etc., cannot be defined in terms of one phrase, "the baptism of the Holy Spirit." Each term needs more exquisite and correct definition and explanation. On the other hand, Kaiser writes as he defines and explains the Baptism of the Holy Spirit:

> How then shall we define the technical term 'baptized in the Holy Spirit? We believe it is best to go with Paul's inspired statement of purpose in 1Corinthian 12:3 that this baptism was the initial work of God of incorporating all believers, first at Pentecost, then in Samaria, and again at Caesarea, into one unified body of Christ in the Holy Spirit. Thereafter, all who believed, at the time of their conversion, were brought by God in the Holy Spirit to join this body and to be part of this one body that is called the believing church of Jesus Christ.[2]

Kaiser is saying that all the believers participate and are united into the body of the Christ and the church through the baptism of the Holy Spirit. As the above definitions show, multiple layers of theological meaning have only added to the confusion.

Ferguson explains from the perspective of the work of Christ:

> This becomes all the clearer when we view Pentecost as an aspect of the work of Christ, not a Spirit event separate from it and in addition to it. It is the visible manifestations of a coronation. The event of the Day of Pentecost are the public expressions of the hidden reality that Christ has been exalted as the Lord of glory and that his messianic request for the Spirit, made as Mediator on our behalf, has been granted.[3]

Ferguson is correct to see the event of Pentecost as the visible manifestation of coronation, a ceremony, but this is not enough to explain the nature of it. It needs more detailed and thorough exegesis to be interpreted from a contextual and redemptive historical perspective.

Accordingly, this writer has taken a different approach to the subject. The basic premise is that there is an error in the translation

2. Kaiser, "Baptism," 31.
3. Ferguson, *Holy Spirit*, 86.

Introduction

of Acts 2:3, and subsequent interpretations and applications have been faulty throughout the long history of Christian theology. The baptism of the Holy Spirit at Pentecost was not an epoch-making event in the redemptive history. Rather, it was simply the installation of Jesus' disciples as new covenant prophets. In support of this proposal, the text in Acts must be examined and explained in terms of its relationship with the events in the Old Testament.

1

The Baptism of the Holy Spirit

The Promise of the Baptism of the Holy Spirit

The risen Christ appeared to his disciples in Jerusalem before his ascension and gave them his final instructions and commissions. After using the scriptures to explain the necessity of his death and resurrection (Luke 24:45–46), he declared that he had been given all authority and that ". . . repentance and forgiveness of sins should be proclaimed in his name to all nations, beginning from Jerusalem" (Luke 24:47). He further commanded them to stay in Jerusalem until they were ". . . clothed with power from on high" (Luke 24:49). In this way, Jesus appointed his disciples to be his worldwide witnesses, and he let them know that they would be empowered by the Holy Spirit to accomplish the mission he had given them. Jesus' command to remain in Jerusalem (Luke 24:48–49) is repeated and expanded in Acts 1:4–5. The promise of the Holy Spirit closes the last scene of the Gospel of Luke and opens the first page of the book of Acts.

While staying with his disciples, Jesus ordered them not to depart from Jerusalem, but to wait for the baptism of the Holy Spirit, the promise of the Father which they heard from him (Acts 1:5). And in verse 8, Jesus again told his disciples that they are to be his witnesses: "You will receive power when the Holy Spirit has come upon you, and you will be my witnesses in Jerusalem and in all Judea and Samaria, and to the end of the earth." In this commandment, Jesus linked the event of Pentecost to his appointment of the disciples as his worldwide witnesses. It should be noted that when Jesus was baptized with water, the Holy Spirit descended on him in bodily form like a dove (Luke 3:22), and this marked the beginning of his messianic ministry. In Acts 1, the disciples were told that they too would receive the Holy Spirit at the outset of their ministry. The Bible refers to this event as "baptism" accompanied with the Holy Spirit. The baptism of the Holy Spirit seemed to be a necessary condition and step in the process of becoming a servant of the Lord, and the event of Pentecost is basically related to the beginning of disciples' ministry of the word.

The Coming of the Holy Spirit

The coming of the Holy Spirit at Pentecost was accompanied by the three unusual phenomena (Acts 2:2–4). First, there was an audible sound like a mighty rushing wind that came from heaven and filled the entire house. There was no actual mighty rushing wind, but rather simply a sound like the wind. The sound seems to have been a signal to capture the attention of the disciples in the room.[1] Since both *ruaḥ* in the Old Testament and *pneuma* in the NT carry double meanings of wind and spirit, and Jesus also compares the Spirit to the wind (John 3:8), the disciples might have recognized this as the appearance and presence of the Spirit coming upon them. In Ezek 37: 9–11, the prophet describes the vision God gave him in which the wind, the breath of the Lord, comes down to the dry bones and breathes new life into them. Thus, the sound of a mighty rushing wind is a fanfare announcing the coming of the Holy Spirit and his presence among the disciples.[2]

---

1. In the Old Testament a wind often follows the presence of God (1 Kgs 19:11; Isa 66:15).

2. Kistemaker and Hendriksen, *Acts*, 75–76. This is not fulfillment of John the Baptist's prophecies of "spirit and power" in Luke 3:16. In that case the fire

The Baptism of the Holy Spirit

Second, there was a visible phenomenon: divided tongues as of fire rested on those who were in the upper room. The Greek text for Acts 2:3, "*kai ōpthēsan autois diamerizomenai glōssai hōsei pyros kai ekathisen ep' hena hekaston autōn*," can be translated as "and the divided tongues as of fire appeared to them and rested on each of them." However, some versions take the translation of "*diamerizomenai glōssai hosei pyros*" to mean "tongues of fire that separated" (NIV). This means that the fire, like divided tongues, came from above and rested on each one of them. This would certainly have been a spectacular and dramatic scene, if it truly happened this way. If this were the case, the fire could possibly refer to God's presence and rest among them (Exod 3:2; 19:18; 1 Kgs 18:38; Ezek 1:27).[3] However, there was no actual fire. Rather, there were "divided tongues like fire." A number of translations convey the correct literal meaning: ESV, "divided tongues like as of fire"; NET, "tongues spreading out like a fire"; NAS, "tongues as of fire distributing themselves"; KJV, "cloven tongues like as of fire." Num 9:15–16 gives us a hint for this translation. There was no fire of cloud, rather "was the appearance of fire on the tabernacle"(*yiheh 'al-hammiškān kᵉmarʾēh-ʾēš*) when it was set up. Calvin translated it as follows: "And they saw cloven tongues, as it were of fire, and it sat upon every one of them."[4] Many modern scholars, however, translate this as the NIV does, drawing various interpretations from it. As he explains the baptism of the Holy Spirit, Gaffin states that "the presence of the fire in the form of a tongue" rested upon the disciples of Jerusalem.[5]

What is the meaning of the cloven tongues coming down to the disciples and why were the tongues in the form of fire? For this answer, we need to remind the scene of God's calling his prophets in the Old Testament.

---

is referring clearly to the judgment. Cf. Luke 3:16; Acts 1:5.

3. Polhill, *Acts*, 98. Lenski translates as "tongues resembling fire," or "fire-like tongues." *Interpretation*, 58–59. Witherington, *Acts*, 132.

4. Calvin, *Acts*, 72–76.

5. Gaffin, *Perspectives*, 17. Marguerat also explains the scene as the flames of fire that come down on each of the Twelve. "Work of the Holy Spirit," 115.

His Touch on the Mouths

Moses was called by the angel of the Lord in a flame of fire out of the midst of a bush that was burning, yet was not consumed (Exod 3:3). The Lord said to him as he turned aside to see the great sight, "Do not come near, take your sandals off your feet, for the place on which you are standing is holy ground." The Lord called Moses in the flame of burning fire on the holy ground. Samuel was called in the house of the Lord, when the lamp of God has not yet gone out (1 Sam 3:3–4).

Isaiah was called in the temple, where the Lord was sitting upon a high and lifted throne and the seraphim were praising and flying around the Lord and the foundation of the threshold was shaking at the voice of him who called and the house was filled with smoke.

Ezekiel saw a divine vision at the Kebar river in the land of Babylonia. He saw a windstorm coming from the north—enormous clouds, with lightning flashing. In the fire were what looked like four living beings with four faces and four wheels. Over the heads of the living beings there was a something like platform and above the platform, which was something like a sapphire-shaped throne. High above on the throne was a form that appeared to be a man. From his waist up was an amber glow like a fire and from his waist down was a brilliant light around it. It looked like the glory of the Lord. This scene of the temple in the universe that Ezekiel saw was more glorious than that of heavenly temple Isaiah saw. Ezekiel was called from this background of universal temple (Ezek 1).

When he began his all-out prophetic ministry, Daniel saw four winds of the sky stirring up the great sea and four large beasts coming up from sea. The heavenly thrones of God were set up and his throne was ablaze with fire and its wheels were all aflame. A river of fire was streaming forth and proceeding from his presence (Dan 7:9–10). From this background he saw "one like a son of man was approaching" with the cloud of the sky.

As we observe the scenes of God calling his prophets, fire or fire-like images accompany them. The glory, grandeur, and impressiveness of the scene of Pentecost remind us of the heavenly temple filled with fire, smoke, and cloud at the time of God's

The Baptism of the Holy Spirit

calling of his prophets. The place where the disciples were gathered together and the Holy Spirit came down with divided tongues like fire seems to be a heavenly temple itself descended upon the scene. G. K. Beale explains the event of Pentecost as follows:

> This is, of course, what happens at Pentecost: not only are the "tongues as of fire" a manifestation of God's presence in the Spirit, but that the presence also causes the people to "prophesy" (as Acts 2:17–18 later makes clear). The location from which God's Spirit descends at Pentecost appear to be not only generally "from heaven" but from the heavenly holy of holies or temple, particularly when seen in light of the descriptions in the OT Sinai theophany, Isa 5 and 30 and the later development of these images in 1 En 14 and 71 and Qumran. Acts 2 appears to be developing these OT images in the same way as 1 Enoch and Qumran. Thus, all these passages together collectively contribute from various vantage points to a picture in Acts 2 that resembles something very like God's fiery theophanic presence as a new heavenly temple extending from heaven and descending on his people and making them a part of it.[6]

If the coming of the Holy Spirit at Pentecost is the coming of the heavenly temple to the earth and Jesus creates his new people as the heavenly temple, as in Beale's theory, it would be an epoch-making event in the redemptive history. However, Beale presupposes the coming of fire at Pentecost. But at Pentecost there was no fire. There was "divided tongues as of fire." The main point of the baptism of the Holy Spirit at Pentecost is not fire, but the divided tongues. The fire referred here is pictorial language, so that it describes the divided tongues as the divided flames of fire. The fire-like imagery of divided tongues in the event of Pentecost

---

6. Beale, *Biblical Theology*, 612. Horton also agrees with Beale at this point: "Rather than cleansing or judgment, the fire here signified God's acceptance of the Church body as the new temple, or sanctuary, of the Holy Spirit (1 Cor 3:16; Eph 2:21–22). Then when the single flames rested on the heads of each individual, it signified accepting them as also being temples of the Spirit (1 Cor 6:19). Thus, the Bible makes clear that the church already in existence before the Pentecostal baptism . . ." Horton, 56–57, quoted in Gaffin, *Perspectives*, 58.

seems to be related to the flames of fire out of the midst of a bush at the time of Moses' call, not with the covenant at Mount Sinai. Thus, Beale's attestation does not fit with Luke's intention that the event of Pentecost is the installation ceremony for the disciples as the new covenant prophets. At Pentecost, there was no fire coming down from above. In his apology that they were not drunkards, Peter did not have any concern about fire. Meyer points out the problem with Luther's understanding of the word and describes his own exposition of the verse:

> After the audible *sēmeion* immediately follows the visible. Incorrectly Luther: "there were seen on them the tongues divided as if they were of fire." The words mean: There appeared to them, i.e. there were seen by them, tongues becoming distributed, fire-like, i.e. tongues which appeared like little flames of fire, and were distributed (2:45; Luke 22:17, 23:34) upon those present (see the following *kathisen, k.t.l.*). They were thus appearance of tongues, which were luminous, but did not burn; not really consisting of fire, but only *hōsei pyros* and not confluent into one, but distributing themselves severally on the assembled. As only similar to fire, they bore an analogy to electric phenomena; their tongue-shape referred as a *sēmeion* to that miraculous *lalein* which ensued immediately after, and the fire-like form to the divine presence (comp. Exod 3:2), which was here operative in a manner so entirely peculiar. The whole phenomenon is to be understood as a miraculous operation of God manifesting Himself in the Spirit, but which, as by preceding sound from heaven, the effusion of the Spirit was made known as divine, and Spirit efficacy on the minds of those who were to receive him was enhanced.[7]

There was no fire, but there were divided tongues that came down upon each one of the disciples. The Greek verb, *opthēsan*, is in plural form when it is used for the appearance of the tongues, but when it is used for "resting on each one of them" the singular

---

7. Meyer, *Critical and Exegetical Handbook*, 1:60–61.

form, *ekadisen*, is used. From this we can deduce that each person was touched with the divided tongues.

Thirdly, there was a feeling of a physical touch and the disciples began to speak in Galilean language, but the people from every nation under heaven heard them speaking in their own language (2:4). The tongue is a speaking organ. It makes sound as the brain orders. Likewise, the disciples did not speak their own thoughts but spoke as the Spirit gave them utterance.

At this sound the multitude came together and were amazed and astonished, saying:

> "Are not all these who are speaking Galileans? And how is it that hear, each of us in his own native language? Parthians and Medes and Elamites and residents of Mesopotamian, Judea and Cappadocia, Pontus and Asia, Phrygia and Pamphylia, Egypt and the parts of Libya belonging to Cyrene, and visitors from Rome, both Jews and proselytes, Cretans and Arabians- we hear them telling in our own tongues the mighty works of God." (Acts 2:7-11)

The people listed here are evidently Jews and reformed Jews from all over the world at that time.

They heard the disciples speaking the great things of God in their own language from where they were living. The disciples spoke in Galilean language and the people that came from other regions heard them in their own languages. There were no translators, no tongues as in Corinthians (1 Cor 14:1–5), no Pentecostal or charismatic tongues. They spoke with simultaneously communicable and understandable languages without translators. Since they had not experienced this kind of phenomena before, they were perplexed and mocked the disciples, saying they were filled with new wine (2:13).

However, Luke writes on these phenomena: "They were filled with the Holy Spirit and began to speak in other tongues as the Spirit gave them utterance." The Greek term *glōssai*, which is translated as "tongue," is used for the organ of speech and taste (Mark 7:33, 35; Luke 16:24; 1 Cor 14:9; Jas 1:26; Rev 16:10), figuratively for a language as a means of verbal communication (Acts 2:11;

Phil 2:11; Rev 5:9), and as a religious technical term for an unintelligible ecstatic utterance (Mark 16:17; 1 Cor 12:10; 13:1, 8, 14).[8] Accordingly, English versions translate the term as "language" (NET, BBE) or "tongue"(ESV, KJV, NIV, NAS, RSV). At Pentecost, the disciples used communicable language without any translators. The term *glōssai* used here was the organ of speech that looked like a divided flame of fire (2:3) and the speech spoken by the disciples was a language as the Spirit gave them utterance. However, the term *glōssai* mentioned in 1 Cor 12–14 is a tongue spoken not to men, but to God. No one understands him because he utters mysteries in the Spirit (1 Cor 14:2) and he needs interpreters (14:27). If we bear in mind the usage of *glōssai*, the disciples who spoke in other languages as the Spirit gave them utterance play the role of YHWH's tongue. In the Old Testament the prophets are called the mouth of the Lord (*pî YHWH*) because they were the spokesman of God. In that sense, the disciples can also be called prophets of the Lord. At this point, we need to examine the relationship between the tongues that came down on the disciples at Pentecost and the prophets as the mouth of God (*pî YHWH*) in the Old Testament. Again, it would be needed to find the meaning of the presence of the tongues upon the disciples, who receive the great commission to make disciples of all nations to the end of this age.

---

8. Danker, *Concise Greek-English Lexicon*; Ginrich, *Greek-English Lexicon*; Friberg et al., *Analytical Greek New Testament*.

2

The Prophets: The Mouth of the Lord

The Spokesman of God

In the Old Testament the Lord appointed the prophets as his spokesmen. Thus, a prophet was called a "man of God" (*'iš haĕlōhîm*)[1] or "the mouth of the Lord" (*pî YHWH*).[2] *Pî YHWH* was used to mean "the commandment of the Lord" (Num 3:16, 39; 4:37, 41; 9:23; Deut 1:26) or "the word of God" (Num 3:16, 17, 51; Deut 34:5; 1 Kgs 13:21, 26). The phrases "the mouth of the Lord, my God" (*pî YHWH ĕlōhî*, Num 22:18) and "the mouth of the Lord, your God" (*pî YHWH ĕlōhêkem*, Deut 1:26; 9:23) are also found.

The Lord called his prophet and gave his words to the prophet to speak. When Moses refused the call from the Lord using the pretext of being slow of speech and tongue, the Lord said, "I will be with your mouth and teach you what you shall speak" (Exod 4:12–13). But Moses was still reluctant to obey, and so the Lord commanded him to go with Aaron, his brother: "You shall speak to him and put the words in his mouth, and I will be with your mouth and with

---

1. Lev 24:2; Deut 8:3; 33:1; 1 Sam 9:7–8; 1 Kgs 12:22; 13:1–34; 14:21, 26, 31; 17:18; 2Kgs 1:12,13; 4:7, 16, 22, 25, 27, 40, 42; 5:8, 14, 15, 20; 6:6, 9; Jer 35:5; Zech 3:2.

2. Lev 24:12; Isa 1:20; 6:7; 40:5; 58:14; 62:2; Jer 5:11; Mic 4:4.

his mouth and will teach you both what to do. He shall speak for you to the people, and he shall be your mouth, and you shall be as God to him" (Exod 4:15–16). Continuing in 7:1–2, God said, "See, I have made you like God to Pharaoh, and your brother Aaron shall be your prophet. You shall speak all that I command you, and your brother Aaron shall tell Pharaoh to let the people of Israel go out of his land." These verses illustrate the relationship between the Lord and Moses and Aaron and Israel (or Pharaoh). God appointed Moses to speak to Pharaoh, and Aaron was the spokesman for Moses. Here the word *nabî'*, translated as "prophet," means "spokesman." Thus, a prophet was the spokesman of God. God was with his prophet and put his words into the mouth of his prophet. Aaron, who was to deliver Moses' words to Pharaoh or to Israel, became like a prophet of Moses, and Moses became like God to Aaron. Likewise, the Lord called Moses and appointed him to be his prophet, to be his spokesman, by putting his words into Moses' mouth.

Later, the Lord promised Moses to give the prophetic institute and said, "I will raise up for them a prophet like you from among their brothers. And I will put my words in his mouth, and he shall speak to them all that I command him" (Deut 18:18). The Lord promised here that he would raise up a prophet like Moses in the future, and he would speak continually to his people through this prophet. Here the phrase "a prophet like you [Moses]" seems to refer to his servants, the prophets, as well as to the great prophet, the Messiah.[3]

In summary, the above passages reveal that the Lord raised up the prophets and put his words into their mouths and let them speak for him. But how did God appoint the prophets?

The Installation of a Prophet

The purpose of God appointing prophets was for them to proclaim his messages to his people and to teach them. God, who created the world by his words, wanted to restore the world by his word

---

3. Young, *My Servants*, 29–35.

The Prophets: The Mouth of the Lord

(Isa 11:1–9; 2:2–5; Ezek 47:1–12; Jer 31:31–34). He wanted to realize his eschatological vision of a peaceful world—a world without war and an earth that filled with the knowledge of the Lord as the waters cover the sea (Isa 11:9). In order to accomplish this, he needed the prophets.

Though God used Adam and Noah as his prophets to reveal his word to his creatures, Abraham was the first person that he actually called a prophet (Gen 20:7). After Moses, the Lord continually called his prophets and put his words in their mouths and commanded them to speak to his people and to teach them (Num 23:5; Isa 51:16; Ezek 2:9—3:2). The process of God's calling and appointment of prophets entailed three steps that are found in the call narratives in the Old Testament.[4]

The first step in the process is God's encounter with the one who was being called. Since the role of prophet was not transmitted by heredity, in contrast to the priestly system, he needed an experience of meeting God. God appeared to the person and called his name, demonstrating his supernatural authority and power, so that the one who was called might have confidence from encountering the divine being. In the case of Moses, God appeared in a flame of fire out of the midst of a bush and called him to be his servant, his prophet, to deliver his people from the bondage of Egypt (Exod 3:1–6). In other instances, God appeared to his soon-to-be-prophet in a vision (Isa 6; Ezek 1–3) or he spoke to the person with words (Jer 1:1–10).

The second step was for God to persuade the one who was called but who was hesitating to answer the call, using an excuse of weakness or poor family background. God disclosed his identity as the God of Abraham, the God of Isaac, and the God of Jacob (Exod 3:6). He explained what he was going to do and gave the person his words to speak to his people. In the calling of Jeremiah, God then touched his hand to Jeremiah's lips and installed him as

---

4. The typical call narrative in the Old Testament is composed of the prophet's encounter with God, God's commission of the task, the prophet's refusal of the call, God's persuasion and proof for the call, and God's promise to be with him. Enne, *Exodus*, 113–20. Plastara, *God of Exodus*, 77–82.

His Touch on the Mouths

his prophet, saying, "Behold, I have put my words in your mouth. See, I have set you this day over nations and over kingdoms, to pluck up and to break down, to destroy and to overthrow, to build and to plant" (Jer 1:9-10). The Lord's touch on Jeremiah's lips was an action that sealed his prophet, signifying that Jeremiah's mouth was God's mouth. Thus, this was actually God's installation ceremony of his prophet who would proclaim the rise and fall of nations and established the authority of the ministry that was to follow. The Lord bestowed on him the authority of a prophet, the servant of his word.[5]

Isaiah saw God sitting on his throne in the heavenly temple, where the angels were continually praising the glory of God. At the sight of this glorious and dazzling scene, Isaiah fell down and fearfully confessed his sinfulness and uncleanness of his lips, just as Moses hid his face when he was called because he was afraid of looking at God (Exod 6:6). Why did Isaiah confess the uncleanness of his lips at this point? The text does not give any explicit answer for this. However, Isaiah seems to be aware of God's calling him as his prophet, as his lips and this could be his reply. Then one of the seraphim flew to him and touched his mouth with a burning coal taken with tongs from the altar, saying, "Behold, this has touched your lips; your guilt is taken away, and your sin atoned for" (Isa 6:6-7). Here the words "mouth" and "lips" are used interchangeably. Traditionally the act of the angel touching Isaiah's mouth has been interpreted as a purifying rite subsequent to his confession of uncleanness.[6] However, this was not simply a rite of purification.

---

5. Calvin comments this as "God stretch out his hand and touched his mouth to show plainly that the prophet's mouth was consecrated to God." Haroutunian, *Calvin*, 377. Huey sees the Lord's touching of Jeremiah's mouth as the action of commissioning him as his spokesman that can be seen in Num 23:5; Deut 18:18; Isa 6:7; 51:16; Ezek 2:29—3:2. Huey, *Jeremiah*, 52. According to Craigie, the divine touch does not symbolize cleansing but rather the imparting of the divine word as Ezekiel ate the scroll and thus made divine word a part of his very being. Thus, the divine word becomes a part of Jeremiah's being. Craigie et al., *Jeremiah 1-25*, 11.

6. Watt says that this is a kind of purifying rite to confer the qualification of the right to speak in the presence of God, who is presiding at his royal court. This is similar to the rite of sacrifice upon entering the temple. But this is a

The Prophets: The Mouth of the Lord

If the action is seen in the context of the call narrative of Isaiah, combined with the knowledge that prophets are usually called "the mouth of the Lord," then the Lord's touching of the lips of Isaiah with a burning coal can be interpreted as an action of appointment that sealed Isaiah as God's official prophet with an assignment to be God's mouthpiece. Thus, the Lord confirmed the calling of the prophet in the presence of the divine beings in his court. The lips of the prophet were not to be unclean, as those of the people were. As a prophet who would speak the word of God, his lips should be clean. Therefore, God's touch on Isaiah's lips with a burning coal seems to have a double meaning: one is a purification rite, and the other is the sealing and installation of his prophet. God, then, sent him with the promise, "I will be with you" (Exod 3:12; Jer 1:19; Matt 28:20).

We can see the same process in the case of Ezekiel. He heard the voice of calling him from the likeness of the glory of the Lord seated on the throne of the heavenly temple, which was over the heads of the living creatures with wings and wheels above the expanse. The appearance of the heavenly temple at the time of Ezekiel's call was more glorious and grandeur than that of Isaiah. Then "the word of the Lord came to Ezekiel the priest, the son of Buzi . . . the hand of the Lord was upon him there" (Ezek 1:3; 3:14, 22).[7] The first encounter of Ezekiel with the Lord is very special. While the word of the Lord came to him, the Lord was touching him with his hands. The Lord was laying his hands on Ezekiel in

---

rite of qualifying and sealing and sending him as a prophet rather than a rite that confers the right to speak at the royal court of the Lord. This is similar to the ceremony for the presidential appointment of an ambassador to a certain country in present days. Horst has explained this well: "In all these cases in which the prophet is allowed to be present through visionary experience during discussions or decisions in the throne room of God, and thus know the 'knowledge of God,' and thus know the 'knowledge of the Almighty,' . . . he is claimed and empowered to make an unusual and overwhelming proclamation—unusual in its shocking harshness or in its great expectation" ("Visionsschiderungen," 198, quoted from Watt, *Isaiah 1–33*, 72). Oswalt. *Isaiah*, 129–30. Motyre, *Isaiah*, 77–78.

7. In the book of Ezekiel, the description "the hand of the Lord was with him" is used when Ezekiel communicates with Lord and sees his visions (1:3; 3:14, 22; 8:1; 37:1; 40:1).

order to appoint him as his prophet. This is obviously a ceremony of installation to commit the mission of the prophet.

Even though the people of Israel rebelled against him, the Lord wanted them that a prophet had been among them. So he wanted to send his prophet to them, whether they hear or refuse, and called Ezekiel:

> "Son of man, eat whatever you find here. Eat this scroll, and go, speak to the house of Israel. So, I opened my mouth and he gave me this scroll to eat. And he said to me, "Son of man, feed your belly with this scroll that I give you and fill your stomach with it." Then I ate it and it was in my mouth as sweet as honey. (Ezek 3:1–3)

When Ezekiel opened his mouth, the Lord put the scroll of the word into his mouth. Here, for "mouth" the Hebrew *peh* is used. YHWH's touching his hands on the mouth with burning coals taken with tongs from the alter, or putting the scroll of the word into his mouth signifies his sealing of the one called to be a prophet who will speak for him.

The third step in the process is for the prophet to go out to be acknowledged by the people as the man from God, the mouth of God. The prophet should then go to the temple or some other public place where he could cry out, "Hear, O Israel, this is the word of God." However, the people would not easily believe the prophet until his identity was confirmed by words or by a demonstration of supernatural power, such as healing, prophesying, or doing miracles. Once he was acknowledged, the people would trust him to be the man of God and would receive and obey his word as the word of God.

The role of prophets in the Old Testament was generally to deliver the messages he received from God to his people, or to interpret and teach it to them. The contents of the message were mainly the coming of the covenantal curses and judgments brought by their rebellion against the covenant made between them, and further hope of restoration. God wanted to establish the new heavens and new earth, which would be full of the knowledge of the Lord as the waters cover the sea (Isa 11:9).

3

The Great Prophet

The New Testament begins with the coming of the great prophet, Jesus Christ. God, the word, incarnated and came as Jesus to this world in order to fill it with the knowledge of the Lord. He came with a prophetic mission to proclaim the word of God and to teach it (Deut 18:18). We can see this from the focus in Jesus' ministry of putting first priority on teaching the people, not on healing the sick, early in the morning (Mark 1:38). This focus is also evident in his prayer on the Mount of Olives in which he reported to God on his ministry of the word prior to his ascension: "For I have given them the words that you gave me, and they have received them and have come to know in truth that I came from you; and they have believed that you sent me" (John 17:8). In this prayer, Jesus recalled that his life has been the life of a prophet. Dunn writes, "Jesus mission can certainly be described as prophetic with proclamation in its reaction against the formalism of contemporary Judaism, and its ministry to the poor."[1]

---

1. Dunn says Jesus was known as a prophet and explains as follows: "First, Jesus had the reputation of prophet even during his life (Mk 6:15 par.; 8:28 pars; 14:65; cf. Matt 21:11, 46; Lk 7:16, 39; 24:19)—the inevitable conclusion to be drawn from his manifest inspiration and authority. Second, Jesus regarded himself as a prophet by his vivid awareness of his anointing and empowering by God's Spirit as in Judaism for the prophets. Third, the mission can certainly be described as prophetic in its proclamation, in his reaction against

His Touch on the Mouths

When Jesus began his ministry as a prophet, he was baptized by John and saw the Spirit like a dove descending upon him. Most scholars define this event, which is recorded in the Synoptic Gospels, as Jesus' inauguration ceremony as the Messiah.[2] The point to be noted here is that Jesus was baptized by water, and the Holy Spirit descended at that moment as he began his ministry of the word. This is obviously a ceremony denoting God's sealing and acknowledgement of him as his prophet. In particular, Luke writes, "And Jesus returned in the power of the Spirit to Galilee, and a report about him went out through all the surrounding country. And he taught in their synagogues, being glorified by all" (Luke 4:14–15). After Jesus received power through baptism, and after he defeated Satan's temptation, he began his mission of teaching the word of God, and he was glorified by all. In this instance, the term glorified means "to be praised," or "to get applause." As it were, it means Jesus was acknowledged by the people as the man of God,

---

the formalism of contemporary Judaism, and its ministry to 'the poor.'" Dunn, *Jesus and the Spirit*, 82–83.

2. Most scholars, such as Bloomberg, regards this event of Jesus' baptism by water and the receiving of the Holy Spirit in Matt 2:15 as being in the royal enthronement context of Ps 2 in what appears here as a formal installation and commissioning. Bloomberg, *Matthew*, 82. Cf. Hagner, *Matthew 1–13*, 58. However, Unger proposed that Jesus' baptism marked "His formal induction into the office of Priest." He writes: "At His baptism Christ received His anointing with the Holy Spirit (Mt 3:16) for his threefold office of prophet, priest, and king which is comprehensively descriptive of His entire ministry. Yet the essence of His redemptive work does not lie in His prophetic or kingly office, but in His consecration as a priest, the Great High Priest, for it was in this office He offered not "the blood of bulls and goats," but Himself in order to put away sin (Heb 9:24–26). It is this consecration to his Priesthood that comes into clearest view in the baptismal scene." Unger, *Baptism*, 51–52. However, though the essence of his redemptive work is the Christ's consecration of his body for the sinners, if it were not for the prophets, who can explain and teach the meaning of it, his death and resurrection would have remained hidden and those sinners who had not heard the gospel would have remained in sin and death. Even though the Christ's death and resurrection is the once-for-all event in history, it is the duty of prophets to teach the effects and meaning of it to the people in order to build the world that is full of the knowledge of the Lord as the waters cover the sea (Isa 11:9). The earthly ministry of Jesus covered almost of all with teaching and training his disciples as the prophet.

The Great Prophet

the prophet. As evidenced in these texts, the relationship between his baptism by the Holy Spirit and the beginning of his ministry cannot be overlooked. Even Jesus required not only God's approval and acknowledgment, but also a positive response from people as he accomplished his prophetic mission from above. When Jesus raised the dead son of widow at the town of Nain, the people followed him show the following response: "Fear seized them all, and they glorified God, saying, 'A great prophet has arisen among us!' And this report about him spread through the whole of Judea and all the surrounding country" (Luke 7:16-17). As Jesus demonstrated his authority in the word and power in raising the dead, the people acknowledged him as "the great prophet," the man from God. However, the Pharisees and the scribes were annoyed at this point. When Jesus taught about heavenly things or performed miracles, they, without fail, asked the source of his authority, identity, and power. "By what authority are you doing these things, or who gave you this authority to do them?" (Mark 11:28; Matt 21:21-27; Luke 20:1-8). Of course, Jesus did not respond to each question. He wanted his people to recognize and believe him through the Scriptures or because of what he was doing or teaching.

However, the situation for his disciples was different. At the beginning of his ministry, he called and trained them "so that they might be with him and he might send them out to preach and have authority to cast out demons" (Mark 3:15). He wanted to give them the prophetical mission to go out to the ends of the earth and to teach them to observe all that they had learned from him (Matt 28:16-20). He had consistent purposes in mind when he chose and called his disciples and when he prayed for them on the Mount of Olives (John 17:18). The disciples needed the same divine authority and power in order to accomplish the mission he gave to them after his resurrection. From this line of continuity, Jesus promised his disciples that he would send them the *parakletos*, which is translated in various ways throughout Scripture: "Comforter" (KJV), "Helper" (TEV, NKJV), "Counselor" (RSV, NIV, HSCB, NLT), or "Advocate" (NSRV). This Helper is the Spirit of truth, the Holy Spirit (John 14:16, 26). By the Father he would be sent to the disciples in the name of Jesus, and they would be in him, and he would be in them, teaching them all things, reminding them of all that he had said to them (20, 26). The Helper would help the disciples to believe, witness, and speak for him (29). The Helper is the one who will assist the disciples in carrying out the prophetic tasks that were commissioned by God. Thus, the Helper was intimately related with the prophetic mission of the disciples. The Helper worked not only for the salvation of each individual sinner in regeneration and sanctification, but he also performed the role of supervisor or supporter as the divine being for the saints to do the work of being a spokesman of God and a witness of Christ.

Jesus called seventy-two disciples and sent them out for evangelical activities.[3] They healed the sick and preached to them, saying, "The kingdom of God has come near to you" (Luke 10:9–10). When they returned with the exciting report of their experience of casting out demons, Jesus responded by saying, "I saw Satan fall like lightening from heaven. Behold, I have given you authority to tread on serpents and scorpions, and over all the power of the enemy, and nothing shall hurt you" (Luke 10:18–19). Jesus reminded them of his support by giving them the authority to control the enemy force that attempted to hinder their ministry. Jesus assumed here the role of being their Helper. However, after Jesus' death, another Helper would assume the role of giving authority and power to the disciples.

---

3. These seventy-two disciples remind us the seventy elders of Israel in Num 11: 13–25. The Lord came down in the cloud and spoke to the people, and he took some of the Spirit that was on Moses and put it on the seventy elders. When the Spirit rested on them, they prophesied, but did not do so again (Num 11:25). Later, Moses gave a hint to Joshua that the Lord appointed those elders as prophets since they prophesied. However, there is textual variance here, where the number is either "seventy" ($\aleph$ A C L W Θ Ξ Ψ $f^{1.13}$ and early versions) or "seventy-two" (P^{75} B D 0181 pc lat and other versions and fathers). Many people preferred to "seventy," although "seventy-two" is more difficult reading and plausible. NET notes, version 1.0.

4

The Great Prophet Appoints His Disciples as Prophets

After his resurrection Jesus came to his disciples and opened (*dianoigō*, Luke 24:31, 32, 45) their eyes (31) and the Scriptures (32), and then opened their minds to understand the Scriptures (45). What is to be noted here, in particular, is that the risen Christ opened the Scriptures in between his resurrection and ascension. His disciples said to each other when he vanished from their sight, "Did not our hearts burn within us while he talked to us on the road, while he opened to us the Scriptures?" (*hōs diēnoigen hēmin tas graphais*, Luke 24:32). Most of English versions translate *diēnoigen* as "opened" (ESV, KJV, ERV, NIV, RSV) rather than "explained" (NET, NAS). Before his leaving Jesus opened the Bible and explained the meaning of his death and resurrection, which has not been disclosed its mysteries yet.[1] Jesus equipped his disciples thoroughly and perfectly in interpreting the Scriptures and its application for the prophetic missions for all nations. He said:

> Thus it is written, that the Christ should suffer and on the third day rise from the dead, and that repentance and forgiveness of sins should be proclaimed in his name to

---

1. Stein, *Luke*, 613. Bock, *Luke 9:51—24:5*, 1920–21.

19

all nations, beginning from Jerusalem. You are witnesses of these things. (Luke 24:46–48)

Matthew writes of Jesus' command to his disciples after his resurrection even more systematically and theologically:[2]

> And Jesus came and said to them, "All authority in heaven and on earth has been given to me. Go therefore and make disciples of all nations, baptizing them in the name of the Father and of the Son and of the Holy Spirit, teaching them to observe all that I have commanded you. And behold, I am with you always, to the end of the age." (Matt 28:18–20)

In this passage, Jesus introduces himself as God, who has all authority in heaven and on earth, and he commands his apostles to make disciples of all nations. The main verb of the command is "to make disciples" (*mathēteusate*), and it is modified by three participles: "going" (*poreuthentes*), "baptizing" (*baptizontes*), and "teaching" (*didaskontes*). This command is followed by the promise that he would be with them until the end of the age. Thus, there are three parts to this conversation:(1) Jesus' self-introduction as God, (2) Jesus' commandment for his disciples to fulfill, and (3) Jesus' promise to be with them. This structure is very similar to the call narrative of the prophets in the Old Testament (Exod 3:1–4:16; Judg 6:11–21; Isa 1–12; Jer 1:4–10).[3] Considering this parallel structure, the passage in Matthew 28 can be viewed as Jesus' appointment of his disciples as prophets, and thus the disciples are the successors of the Old Testament prophets, who were the spokesmen for God in the history of redemption. They became "the new mouth of God," a role that necessitated the sealing of God with prophetic authority and power. Therefore, Jesus promised the coming of the Helper and sent him at Pentecost.

---

2. Nolland, *Matthew*, 1261.
3. Hagner, *Matthew 12–28*, 883.

The Great Prophet Appoints His Disciples as Prophets

The Baptism of the Holy Spirit

Before Jesus sent the Helper, the Holy Spirit, Jesus promised that although John had baptized his followers with water, his disciples would be baptized with the Holy Spirit in just a few days (Acts 1:5). Jesus compares the coming baptism of the Holy Spirit with his previous baptisms by water. At the time of his baptism by John, the Holy Spirit came down and witnessed his identity as the Son of God, the Messiah. Therefore, the baptism of water accompanied by the baptism of the Holy Spirit can be viewed as the inaugural ceremony of his prophetic ministry as the Messiah.

Likewise, the disciples of Jesus needed this same procedure. They were about to begin a ministry of the word that Jesus commissioned to them, and they were in need of confirming their identity of prophet by the Holy Spirit as Jesus did. Therefore, the baptism of the Holy Spirit can be regarded as an installation ceremony sealing the disciples of Jesus with the Holy Spirit as prophets and bestowing them with authority and power.

The appearance of divided tongues like those of fire that came down upon the disciples in this "ceremony" can be regarded as similar to the incidents when God touched the mouths of Isaiah and Jeremiah as a symbol of his seal upon them, declaring, "You are my mouth."

At this point, Calvin teaches that God divided and clove the tongues of the apostles for the purpose of preaching the gospel to the nations of the world. But he does not mention God's sealing of the apostles as new covenant prophets. He expounds Acts 2:3 as follows:

> The diversity of tongues did hinder the gospel from being spread abroad any farther; so that, if the preachers of the gospel had spoken one language only, all men would have thought that Christ had been shut up in the small corner of Jewry. But God invented a way whereby it might break out, when he divided and clove the tongues of the apostles, that they might spread that abroad amongst all people which was delivered to them. Wherein appeareth the manifold goodness of God, because a plague and

punishment of man's pride was turned into a matter of blessing. For whence came the diversity of tongues, save only that the wicked and ungodly counsels of men might be brought to naught? (Gen. 11:7.) But God doth furnish the apostles with the diversity of tongues now, that he may bring and call home, into a blessed unity, men which wander here and there. These cloven tongues made all men to speak the language of Canaan, as Isaiah foretold (Isa. 19:18). For what language soever they speak, yet do they call upon one Father, which is in heaven, with one mouth and one spirit (Rom. 15:6).[4]

Calvin's understanding of the divided tongues was correct, but he did not relate the divided tongues with "the mouth of the Lord" (*pî YHWH*), the prophet of the Lord in the Old Testament. The mouth cannot speak by its own willpower. The tongue can only utter a sound or language as the brain gives orders to it. The disciples, as the mouth of the Lord, "began to speak in other tongues as the Spirit gave utterance" (Acts 2:3). There is no need to distinguish here between "mouth" and "tongues." David said in his last words, "The Spirit of the Lord speaks by me; his word is on my tongue" (*ruaḥ YHWH dibbel-bî umillaṯōw ʿal-lĕšōwnî*, 2 Sam 23:2). David's statement here well expresses the relationship between the Spirit, the word, and tongues.[5] David used the word for "tongue" instead of "mouth" in describing the member of the body that is used to speak for God. "Mouth" and "tongue" are synonyms and are used interchangeably in the Bible. When the disciples spoke in tongues, there were no translators. Everyone that came from a foreign country could hear the disciple's sayings without the help of a translator. Their tongues were in communicable languages without translators.

---

4. Calvin, *Acts*, 75.
5. Bergen, *1, 2 Samuel*, 465–66.

The Great Prophet Appoints His Disciples as Prophets

Peter's Understanding of the Baptism of the Holy Spirit

It is important to note how Peter and other disciples who received the baptism of the Holy Spirit understood it. Peter tried to prove to the mocking crowds that he and his comrades were not drunkards. He testified that they were the prophets of God by outpouring of the Holy Spirit, who was sent by Jesus, who was killed by the Jews but was resurrected by God. The main theme of Peter's long speech in Acts 2:14–39 was not to prove Jesus' resurrection, but rather to give witness to their status as prophets from above.[6] To do this, Peter quoted from the prophet Joel.

> And it shall come to pass afterward,
> that I will pour out my spirit upon all flesh;
> and your sons and your daughters shall prophesy [wĕnibbĕ'û]
> your old men shall dream dreams,
> and your young men shall see visions. (Joel 2:28)

---

6. Dodd notes six points that, he says, form a pattern common to the speeches in Acts as a whole. Followings are summary of his six points: (1) The age of fulfilment has dawned. (2) This has taken place through the life, death, and resurrection of Jesus, of which a brief account is given. (3) By virtue of the resurrection, Jesus has been exalted at the right hand of God, as messianic head of the new Israel. (4) The Holy Spirit in the church is the sign of Christ's present power and glory. (5) The messianic age will shortly reach its consummation in the return of Christ. (6) The preaching always closes with an appeal for repentance, the offer of forgiveness and of the Holy Spirit, and the promise of salvation to those who enter the elect community. Dodd, "Apostolic Preaching and Its Development," 21–24, quoted in Barrett, *Acts*, 130–32. Many scholars have acknowledged, as Dodd alleged, that this is a theological sermon with the typical six forms and elements in Acts testifying to Jesus' death and resurrection. However, the literary structure of the text shows that the death and resurrection of Jesus is a necessary element in order to prove the identity of the Holy Spirit who sealed them as prophets. Peter is saying, as it were, that they became new covenant prophets by the sealing of the Holy Spirit sent by Jesus Christ, who asked it of God, and then the disciples spoke in tongues in order to prove their status as "the spokesmen of God," the prophets.

His Touch on the Mouths

According to Joel, God would pour out his Spirit on all flesh in the last days and they would prophesy, see visions, and dream dreams (Joel 2:28; Acts 2:17). Peter adds here the phrase:

> And on my servants and on my handmaidens
> I will pour out in those days of my Spirit [*ekcheō apo tou pneumatos mou*],
> and they will prophesy (*prophēteúsousin*). (Acts 2:18)

This Spirit would be poured out even on his male servants and female servants, who would also prophesy (Acts 2:18). Peter is saying that the prophecy of Joel is now fulfilled among themselves as the Holy Spirit came and they spoke in different languages. Peter regards their speaking in different languages as prophesying.

Joel's prophecy was rooted in the occurrence in Numbers 11:24–30 when God responded to Moses' complaint about the burden of responsibility he had in caring for Israel, his people, by appointing seventy elders to be Moses' assistants. The Lord took some of the Spirit that was on Moses and put it on the seventy elders who were standing around the tent. When the Spirit rested on them, the result was that they prophesied (Num 11:24–25). But there were two other men, Eldad and Medad, who were among the registered but were not physically present with the seventy who also prophesied. Joshua asked Moses to stop them, but Moses replied, "Are you jealous for my sake? Would that all the Lord's people were prophets, that the Lord would put his Spirit on them!" (Num 11:29). It is to be noted that God gave the same Spirit to the seventy and appointed them to be Moses' aids to do the same work with him and let them prophesy as an acknowledgment of their status as prophets. However, the details of their prophesying are unknown—how they prophesied, whether or not they spoke in tongues, whether they fell in ecstasy as King Saul did when he prophesied, etc. The purpose of prophesying was to appoint elders to a certain office for a limited time. Subsequently, Moses refers to the prophesying elders as "prophets."[7]

---

7. Cole points out that the outpouring of the Spirit upon the seventy elders and following prophecy show the pattern of God's working of appointing his

The Great Prophet Appoints His Disciples as Prophets

Joel's prophecy is similar to this event in its nature. The only difference is in the terms "all the Lord's people" (*kāl-'am YHWH*, Num 11:29) and "all flesh" (*kāl bāšal*, Joel 2:28). Joel states that God will give his Spirit to all the people, and they will be prophets. "All flesh" refers to all the people, without distinctions of race, nationality, age, gender, etc. It would not be limited to Israel, the Lord's people. Thus, the prophecy of Joel seems to contain historical, worldwide, and further universal meanings.[8] Accordingly, God wanted to appoint all the people of the world to be his prophets by giving them his Spirit. Both Moses' words and Joel's prophecy, then, deal with the promise of God's appointment and installation of all people as prophets in the last days by an outpouring of his Spirit upon them.

Peter, by quoting the verses from Joel, was stating that the prophecy was now fulfilled. The phrase "and they shall prophesy" (Acts 2:18) when God pours out his Spirit should be particularly noted. This is an addition to the text Peter quoted from Joel. He seemed to apply it to himself with the understanding that he had been given the office of prophet, not simply that he had received the Holy Spirit. Peter went on to explain that it was Jesus who had given the disciples the Holy Spirit (Acts 2:22–36). Even though the Israelites had killed the one whom God sent, God raised him from the dead and exalted him as was prophesied by David. Therefore, the point Peter made here is that the disciples were prophesying because Jesus, risen from the dead, poured out the Holy Spirit upon them, just as Joel had prophesied. From the structural analysis of this text, it is evident that the main point of Peter's speech was not the resurrection of Jesus, but rather that Peter and the other disciples are the prophets that were referred to by Moses and foretold by Joel in the Scriptures. This self-justification by Peter cut the listening crowd of people in Jerusalem to the heart, and they

---

servants, the prophets among his people. *Numbers*, 193.

8. Peter's understanding of this prophecy of Joel was very much in keeping with the rabbinic consensus that the Spirit no longer rested only on Israel, but that it would return as a universal gift at the end time. Barrett, *Acts*, 136. Polhill, *Acts*, 108.

His Touch on the Mouths

responded to Peter and the rest of the apostles by asking, "Brothers, what shall we do?" (Acts 2:37). John the Baptist was asked this same question by the crowd when they heard his preaching of repentance (Luke 3:10). Their questions reveal that they acknowledged both John and the apostles as prophets. Therefore, Peter's speech is neither mainly about the resurrection of Jesus, nor the proclamation of the coming of a new age.[9] The disciples regarded themselves as prophets appointed by Jesus and sealed by the Holy Spirit of God.

If this understanding of the text is correct, the baptism of the Holy Spirit at Pentecost was actually the installation ceremony that sealed the disciples by the Holy Spirit as the new covenant prophets. Thus, the baptism of the Holy Spirit was not given for the regeneration of sinners or for the sanctification of the saints, but rather, it was an event that sealed the disciples as the mouth of God, bestowing upon them the necessary authority and power to be witnesses to the word of God to the ends of the earth. The Greek work *spragizō* means "to mark (as with a seal) to identify." In John 6:26, the act of sealing is a confirmation of the identity of God's Son by sealing him as the one who would give the food that endures to eternal life. Another example of this sealing can be found in Paul's words to the Corinthians: "And it is God who establishes us with you in Christ, and has anointed us, and who has also put his seal on us and given us his Spirit in our hearts as a guarantee" (2 Cor 1:21-22). The Greek *bebaiōn* is a juristic term whose meaning is "to establish" or "to confirm to be effective."[10] An anointing was a symbolic act when a priest poured oil on the head of a king or priest on behalf of God in order to install and confirm his office (1 Sam 10:1; 16:13; 1 Kgs 1:39). Similarly, Paul is saying that God has appointed him and the Corinthians as his servants, giving the Holy Spirit in their hearts as a seal and guarantee in order to confirm the appointment. Thus, both the anointing of oil and sealing by the pouring out of the Holy Spirit are God's acts of appointing his servants and guaranteeing their status.

---

9. Menzies, *Development*, 224-29. Atkinson, *Baptism*, 52-53.
10. Murray, *2 Corinthians*, 205.

The Great Prophet Appoints His Disciples as Prophets

Further confirmation of the disciples' position is found in Hebrews 2:4: "While God also bore witness by signs and wonders and various miracles and by gifts of the Holy Spirit[11] distributed according to his will." The signs and wonders and miracles shown by the disciples testify to their position as servants of God (2 Cor 12:12; Rom 15:19). The disciples' ability to speak in tongues at Pentecost also testified that God had appointed them and that he was using them for his purpose.[12]

The Disciples Acknowledged as the New Covenant Prophets

The disciples were mocked as drunkards by the people of Jerusalem. Peter and John rose up against them and justified their identity as the new covenant prophets through the long speech based on the Scriptures. In the following speech we can observe the responses of the people. One group was by three thousand ordinary people of Jerusalem and those who came from the overseas, and the other group of five thousand peoples with the religious and various kind of social leaders. The disciples needed the acknowledgement of their prophetical office from the people of God in order to accomplish their mission given by Jesus Christ.

Acknowledgement by Three Thousand People

When the prophets were called and sent by God in the Old Testament, they were to be acknowledged as men sent from God by their words and deeds in order to do the mission of prophets. Moses was worried about this authority being recognized, and he said to God, "But they will not believe me or listen to my voice, for they will say, 'The Lord did not appear to you'" (Exod 4:1). God then enabled him to perform first the miracle of changing a

---

11. The Greek text does not mention the "the gifts" here and reads πνεύματος ἁγίου μερισοῖς ("and distributions of the Holy Spirit").

12. Poythress, "Baptism."

staff into a serpent and then striking his hand with leprosy before restoring it to complete health. God said to him, "If they will not believe you, or listen to the first sign, they may believe the latter sign." (4:8). God told him to show miracles to the people so that he could be acknowledged as the "man of God." Likewise, the prophets were acknowledged as men from God by their words which were fulfilled and the supernatural works that they performed. When Elijah raised the widow's son to life, she said, "Now I know that you are a man of God, and that the word of the Lord in your mouth is truth" (1Kgs 17:24). This seems to be the general process for prophets to receive acknowledgment from the people that they are prophets of the Lord. Even Jesus and John the Baptist were questioned as to their source of authority and power that enabled them to do supernatural works (Matt 11:3; Lk 7:18–23). Many who heard Jesus' teaching said, "Where did this man get these things? What is the wisdom given to him? How are such mighty works done by his hands? Is not this the carpenter, the son of Mary and brother of James and Joses and Judas and Simeon? And are not his sisters here with us?" (Mark 6:2–3).

The disciples of Jesus also required this process of acknowledgement in order to work as new covenant prophets. We see here two stages for disciples to receive acknowledgement from the people. The first stage was evidenced by three thousand people on the day they received the baptism of the Holy Spirit at Pentecost after Peter's speech defending their divine prophetship in Acts 2. The second stage of recognition was by the five thousand people and many religious and political dignitaries of Jerusalem after Peter healed a man lame from birth, as recorded in Acts 3 and 4.

On the day of Pentecost, the disciples were baptized by the Holy Spirit and spoke in a different language, and the devout Jews dwelling in Jerusalem from every nation under heaven were amazed and perplexed and even mocked them as drunkards (Acts 2:13). Peter testified his identity as a new covenant prophet, and the people who heard him were cut to the heart and asked, "Brothers, what shall we do?" (Acts 2:37). This is the question that was raised of the prophets in the Old Testament and of John the Baptist (Luke

The Great Prophet Appoints His Disciples as Prophets

3:10) and Jesus in the New Testament when the people recognized them as men sent from God. Thus, this question can be regarded as the mark of people's recognition of someone as a prophet sent from God.[13]

Peter replied that the listeners should repent and be baptized in the name of Jesus for the forgiveness of sins, and then they would receive the gift of the Holy Spirit. They accepted his words and were baptized, and approximately three thousand souls were added to the church on that day (2:41). However, it must be noted that there is no mention that these three thousand spoke in tongues when they were baptized. Although they must have received the gift of the Holy Spirit as Peter instructed, no visible signs were seen, nor were audible sounds heard.[14] However, the recipients accepted the apostles as prophets. Peter did not tell them to receive the baptism of the Holy Spirit. He obviously made distinction between the baptism of the Holy Spirit and the gift of the Holy Spirit (*hē dōrea tou hagiou pneumatos*). The baptism of the Holy Spirit is a ceremony for the installation of the new covenant prophet. It is exclusively used in the New Testament for giving the office of prophet, for Jesus' baptism by John (Mark 1:8) and for the disciples at Pentecost (Acts 1:5). However, the gift of the Holy Spirit that Peter mentioned in his instruction to the people (Acts

---

13. Similar questions are raised by the crowds in 10:25; 18:18 (par. Mark 10:17); John 6:28; Acts 2:37; 16:30; 22:10. In each case it is asked by persons seeking salvation or wishing to know God's will for their lives. Marshall, *Luke*, 142.

14. The gift of the Holy Spirit that Peter mentioned in his instruction to the people (Acts 2:38) was for their salvation, not for their ordination of prophetic office. Friberg's lexicon explains that the gift of the Holy Spirit "in the New Testament is only used for spiritual and supernatural gifts that are freely given by God to believers, including eternal life (Jn 4:10), the Holy Spirit (Acts 2:38), righteousness, i.e. state of being put right with God (Rom 5:17), enabling grace for appointed ministry (Eph 3:7)." Friberg et al., *Greek Lexicon*. Gaffin, however, states, "the gifts (plural) of the Spirit are not 'means of grace' in the sense of those provisions of God—Scripture, the sacraments and prayer—which are intended for all believers and are indispensable for personal sanctification and growth in grace. No one gift (*e.g.*, tongues) is necessary for the worship and witness God desires in each one of this people." Gaffin, "Holy Spirit," 74.

2:38) was for their salvation, not for their ordination of prophetic office.

Acknowledgement by Five Thousand with the Religious Leaders

Peter and John healed the man who was lame from the birth at the Beautiful Gate of the temple (Acts 3:1–10). All the people who saw him walking and praising God were filled with wonder and amazement at what had happened to him, and they gathered to Peter and John in Solomon's Portico. Peter again addressed the crowd with a long speech about the source of their power, i.e., the name of Jesus Christ. Many of those who heard his preaching believed, and the number of the men came to about five thousand (Acts 4:4). Because of this incident, Peter and John were put into custody and taken to the seat of interrogation before the various political and religious dignitaries in Jerusalem, such as rulers, elders, scribes, Annas the high priest, and John and Alexander the high-priestly family. These leaders asked Peter what the source of their authority and power was (7). Peter boldly explained how the crippled man was healed by the name of Jesus Christ of Nazareth and exhorted them to believe in him (8–12). When they first saw the disciples, they perceived that they were uneducated common men. But they were ultimately astonished at their boldness and recognized that they were the disciples of Jesus when they saw the man who was healed standing beside them. They could say nothing in opposition, and they conferred with one another, saying, "What shall we do with these men? For that a notable sign has been performed through them is evident to all the inhabitants of Jerusalem, and we cannot deny it" (13–14). They could not help but acknowledge them as men of God, the prophets who were sent by him.

The baptism of the three thousand at Pentecost by the disciples and the rulers of the people and the elders' indisputable acceptance of the disciples after their interrogation regarding the source of the apostle's authority and power to heal the man who was lame from the birth, were the events demonstrating and confirming the

The Great Prophet Appoints His Disciples as Prophets

identity of the disciples as the new covenant prophets. Accordingly, the baptism of three thousand people at Pentecost in Acts 2 and the baptism of five thousand people in Acts 3–4 are not same in character. Luke seems to have in mind that the disciples were acknowledged as the prophets of new covenant by all classes of people. Through these two incidents, they could not find nor say anything against their prophetic ministry, which had been commissioned by Jesus. The signs and wonders and miracles shown by the disciples testified to their identity as the servants of God (2 Cor 12:12; Rom 15:19). The book of Hebrews further comments and explains the witness of God for his prophets: "While God also bore witness by signs and wonders and various miracles and by gifts of the Holy Spirit distributed according to his will" (Heb 2:4; cf. 2 Cor 12:12; Rom 15:19).[15]

---

15. Poythress, "Baptism."

5

The Activities of the New Covenant Prophets

After Pentecost, how did the disciples accomplish the great commission of Jesus as the new covenant prophets and how did the Helper he promised work with them? Before we proceed to the subject, we need to search the reason for the Christ's purpose to appoint his disciples to be the prophets of the world from the redemptive historical perspective.

God's Vision of New Creation

God planned to restore the fallen world through the word of God. The Bible tells the state of the world after the fall of Adam:

> "For they deliberately overlook this fact, that the heavens existed long ago, and the earth was formed out of water and through water by the word of God, and that by means of these the world that then existed was deluged with water and perished. But by the same word the heavens and earth that now existed are stored up for fire, being kept until the day of judgment and destruction of the ungodly." (2 Pet 3–7)

The Activities of the New Covenant Prophets

According to these verses, the heavens and earth were created by the word of God and are preserved for fire and kept until the day of judgment and destruction. At the time of Noah, it was destroyed by water, but on the day of judgment it will be perished by fire. Thus, by the word of God the world was created and the judgment and destruction on the last day will be accomplished. God began history by his word and will finish it by his word too. Since this world created by the word and the fall of the world was also brought by man's disobedience of the word, it is evident that the restoration should also come through the word of God. The restoration of this fallen world will be the world of the word, the word of the Lord that reigns over the world as at creation. The order of the Lord will be established, and man will fear the Lord and obey his word. On that day the word will flourish over the world and peace will be settled on earth (Isa 2:1–4; 11:1–9; 31:31–34; 65:17–25; Ezek 47, etc.). God told and showed this vision of restoration to his prophets and commanded them to speak and teach his people for him. God called Abraham to be the father of Israel and told him the purpose of his call.

> Shall I hide from Abraham what I am about to do, seeing that Abraham shall surely become a great and mighty nation, and all the nations of the earth shall be blessed in him? For I have chosen him, that he may command his children and his household after him to keep the way of the Lord by doing righteousness and justice, so that the Lord may bring to Abraham what he has promised him. (Gen 18:17–19)

Here the word "way of the Lord" is also used in the Bible for "the order of his lips," "the word of his lips," "the law of the Lord," "the rules and statues of the Lord" (Ps 18:21–22).

The "way" in the metaphorical sense conveys the idea of life style or pilgrimage.[1] "The way of the Lord" indicates a life whose conduct conforms to the prescription of the Lord, particularly observing the stipulations of the covenant and showing loyalty

---

1. Koch, "דרך, derek," *TDOT*, 3:282–93. Merrill, "דרך" *NIDOTTE*, 1:989–93.

to the Lord (Deut 8:6; 9:12; Judg 2:22; 2 Kgs 21:22).[2] The command to teach and keep the word of God is found very often in the Scriptures (Exod 12:25–27; Deut 6:12–13, 20–25; Prov 1:7; 13:1, etc.). The purpose of his choosing Abraham, God said, was so that Abraham and his children would keep and obey the word of God and do justice and righteousness, and all the nations would be blessed through him. God wanted to build the new world through Abraham, the world of the word and justice and righteousness. God wanted to make the fallen man and the world revive with the word. God choose Israel, the sons of Abraham, for his people and gave his laws and commandments to them to be his kingdom of priests and revealed the same plan to them through his prophets.

In Isaiah 11, God shows the vision of the restored world in which all kind of animals, such as the wolf, lamb, leopard, young goats, lion, fattened calf, cow, ox, nursing child, cobra, etc., renounce their ingrained hostilities and live together (Isa 11:6–8). This will be realized when the earth is full of the knowledge of God as the waters covered the sea (Isa 11:9). And Isa 2:1–4 shows the picture of all the nations flowing to the highest mountain of the house of the Lord and saying:

> "Come, let us go up to the mountain of the Lord,
> to the house of the God of Jacob,
> that he may teach us his ways [*midděrākāyw*]
> and that we may walk in his paths."
> For out of Zion shall go the law,
> and the word of the Lord from Jerusalem. (Isa 2:2–3)

Zion and Jerusalem are described as the places where the house of the Lord is located, and the word of the Lord flows down from there and the peoples stream to receive it. The laws and words here, of course, are referring to the words that the Lord had given to his people through his servants, such as Moses and other prophets. It is to be noted that "the ways of the Lord" (*delek YHWH*), used in the context of informing the purpose of his calling of Abraham in Genesis, is also used in the phrases "the paths taught from the

2. Mathews, *Genesis 11:27–50:26*, 224.

The Activities of the New Covenant Prophets

house of the Lord," "the law from Zion," "the word of the Lord from of Jerusalem," and "the way of the Lord." This scene of all the nations going up to the house of the Lord to be taught by his word is not without relation with the Jesus' ministry of the word and his disciples afterward in the redemptive history. The peoples shall beat all kinds of weapons into agricultural instruments and peace will be settled on earth as described in Isaiah 11.

At this moment, we need to turn our attention to the vision of Ezekiel 47. The water was issuing from below the threshold of the temple and flew to the four quarters of regions and made every creature alive.

> Then he brought me back to the door of the temple, and behold, water was issuing from below the threshold of the temple toward the east (for the temple faced east). The water was flowing down from below the south end of the threshold of the temple, south of the altar. . . . when the water flows into the sea, the water will become fresh. And wherever the river goes, every living creature that swarms will live, and there will be very many fish. For this water goes there, that the waters of the sea may become fresh, so everything will live where the river goes. . . . And on the banks, on both sides of the river, there will grow all kinds of trees for food. Their leaves will not wither, nor their fruit fail, but they will bear fruit every month, because the water for them flows from the sanctuary. Their fruit will be for food, and their leaves for healing. (Ezek 47:1, 8–9, 12)

Whereas in Isaiah the nations go up to the temple on the mountain of the Lord flowing the word of God in order to receive it, in Ezekiel the water flowing from the threshold of the temple went to the river and finally entered into the sea and made every creature live. It reminds us of the scene of a river out of Eden to water the garden and eventually whole world (Gen 2:10) and the river of water of life flowing from the throne of God and of the Lamb (Rev 22:1–5). The water of life flowing from the throne of God and of Lamb fight off the power of death and make all creatures live. The image of water flowing from the temple is found

35

very often in the Scriptures (Ps 36:8; 46:4; Joel 3:18; Zech 13:1; 14:8 etc.). If the temple is a type of Christ, the water flowing from the temple will be regarded as the water flowing from Christ. Christ Jesus told the Samaritan woman, "whoever drinks of the water that I will give him will never be thirsty again. The water that I will give him will become in him a spring of water welling up to eternal life" (John 4:14). And in John 7:37–38 he said, "If anyone thirst, let him come to me and drink. Whoever believes in me as the Scripture has said, 'Out of his heart will flow rivers of living water.'" John, one of his disciples, interpret the phrase as "Now this he said about the Spirit, whom those who believed and in him were to receive, for as yet the Spirit had not been given, because Jesus was not yet glorified" (John 7:39). Therefore, the water flowing from the temple is referring to the Holy Spirit that will be given by Christ Jesus.

From this we can see here that both the word and Spirit simultaneously flow from the temple, from Jesus. Since the word and Spirit come from the body of Christ, they are not separable and always work together. Where the word is proclaimed the Holy Spirit works, and the Holy Spirit works through the word.[3] We cannot bring the Holy Spirit and control it, but we can proclaim the word of God and teach it. Then the Spirit works through the word we preach. By this, the disciples can participate in the work of God to realize the vision of the last day that the knowledge of the Lord will fill the earth as the waters cover the sea. Thus, the Lord give the eternal covenant through Isaiah:

> "And as for me, this is my covenant with them," says the LORD: "My Spirit that is upon you, and my words that I have put in your mouth, shall not depart out of your mouth, or out of the mouth of your offspring, or out of the mouth of your children's offspring," says the LORD, "from this time forth and forevermore." (Isa 59:21)

Jeremiah also writes of the same vision of the new covenant:

> For this is the covenant that I will make with the house of Israel after those days, declares the LORD: I will put my

---

3. Calvin, *Institutes*, IX.3.

The Activities of the New Covenant Prophets

> law within them, and I will write it on their hearts. And I will be their God, and they shall be my people. And no longer shall each one teaches his neighbor and each his brother, saying, "Know the LORD," for they shall all know me, from the least of them to the greatest, declares the LORD. For I will forgive their iniquity, and I will remember their sin no more. (Jer 31:34)

The eschatological vision of restoration is to establish a new world where the word of God reigns and prevails, and as a result peace will settle on earth and there will be no war.

God appointed the prophets to realize this vision and put his word into their mouth in order to speak for him among his people and teach them. Now his time has been fulfilled. God, the word himself made flesh, came into this world as Christ and began to preach and teach his word. The multitude of people listened to his word and followed him.

They regarded him as the great prophet promised in the Old Testament. The twelve disciples confessed Jesus as the Lord and Christ and were trained by him as his prophets. Jesus' ministry of the word grew enough to draw attention from his people all throughout the country, now among those Greeks who came to Jerusalem to worship at the feast and visited Jesus (John 12:20). Jesus seemed to regard the presence of the Gentiles as the fulfillment of the prophecy given through Isaiah (Isa 2:1–4 and 11:6–9). At their appearance, he recognized it was time for his departure from this world and to hand over his ministry of the word to his disciples.[4] He said to them, "Truly, truly I say to you, unless a grain of wheat falls into the earth and dies, it remains alone; but if it dies, it bears much fruit" (John 12:24). Jesus here compares himself to a grain of wheat and we can see many of these examples comparing the word to seed (Mark 4:14; 1 Pet 1:23). Accordingly, the word will fall into the earth and then the seed of the word will sprout and bear much fruit. Jesus is teaching the meaning of his death and resurrection to his disciples from the perspective of the word in the redemptive history. From this point on, Jesus promised his

---

4 Borchert, *John 12–21*, 49.

disciples to give them the Helper (14:26; 15:26; 16:7). Afterward, he appointed and sealed his disciples by the Holy Spirit to be his successors of prophetic ministry of the word.

Disciples' Ministry of the Word as the New Covenant Prophets

The command of the risen Christ to his disciples was to make disciples of all nations by baptizing and teaching them to observe all that he commanded (Matt 28:16–20). Before his ascension, he instructed them to go out to Jerusalem, all Judea and Samaria, and the ends of the earth (Acts 1:8). By this command, his disciples went out to obey and accomplish the mission they received. It is our turn to trace the activities of new covenant prophets after they were baptized by the Holy Spirit.

Peter and John at Jerusalem

The disciples of Jesus had to prove their identity as the new covenant prophets, because the people regarded them as drunkards when they heard them speaking in tongues (actually different languages) after their baptism of the Holy Spirit at Pentecost. At this critical situation, Peter stood up and gave to them a self-justifying speech that he and the disciples were baptized by the Holy Spirit at Pentecost. Peter emphasized that "This Jesus God raised up and of that we are all witnesses. Being therefore exalted at the right hand of God and having received from the Father the promise of the Holy Spirit, he has poured out this that you yourselves are seeing and hearing" (Acts 2:32–34). The response of the people to Peter's speech was, "Brothers, what shall we do?" This same question was asked by the peoples to John the Baptist when he preached the baptism of repentance (Luke 3:10). This suggests that the people who heard Peter's speech identified him with the prophet John the Baptist. Peter gave them same answer, "Repent and be baptized . . ." (Acts 2:38). On that day about three thousand souls were baptized.

The Activities of the New Covenant Prophets

Furthermore, in Acts 3–4 Peter and John healed a man lame since birth at the Beautiful Gate of the temple. They demonstrated their identity not only by their speech but also by their power of doing miracles, and about five thousand people believed after this event. The political rulers and all the religious leaders and social dignitaries of Jerusalem inquired of the disciples about their source of authority and power and conferred with one another, saying, "What shall we do with these men?" However, they had nothing to say against the apostles because of their educated, eloquent speech and evidences. They had to accept them as the new covenant prophets.

It is to be noted here in these events that there is no mention of three thousand or five thousand people speaking in tongues when they were baptized. Peter said that they would be given "the gift of the Holy Spirit" from God if they repented and were baptized. The Holy Spirit was given to the disciples and the gift of the Holy Spirit, he said, would be given to the people of three tousand and five thousand. Those who repented and believed now needed the gift of salvation, not the baptism of the Holy Spirit in order to be prophets. The gift of the Spirit was given for them to become members of the new covenant people, for those heard and believed the disciples' teaching and repented were baptized and saved.

Being recognized by the all classes of people in Jerusalem, the activities of the disciples proceeded forward without obstacle and the number of believers multiplied. Luke reports: "And devoted themselves to the apostle's teaching and fellowship, to the breaking of bread and the prayers" (Acts 2:42). Obviously, the disciples' activities were focused on prophetic teaching and learning. After the event of healing the lame from the birth at the Beautiful Gate, the disciples became more bold and courageous in their prophetic activities and they became more confident in their mission given by the Lord Jesus.

> "And now, Lord, look upon their threats and grant to your servants to continue speaking your word with all boldness, while you stretch out your hand to heal, and signs and wonders are performed through the name of

His Touch on the Mouths

your holy servant Jesus." And when they had prayed were all filled with the Holy Spirit and continued to speak the word of God with boldness. (Acts 4:29-31)

The disciples were all filled with the Holy Spirit and proclaimed the word of God. With this teaching activities, many signs and wonders were regularly done among people by the hands of the apostles (5:12). The multitudes of people from the towns around Jerusalem gathered to the Lord, and the sick and those afflicted with unclean spirits were brought and carried into the streets and laid on cots and mats, so that as Peter passed by at least his shadow might fall on some of them (5:12-16).

As the ministry of the disciples grew and expanded, the priests and Sadducees were filled with jealousy and rose up and arrested the disciples and put them into the public prison. But during the night an angel of the Lord opened the prison doors and brought them out and said, "Go and stand in the temple and speak to the people all words of this Life" (5:20). This reminds us of when Daniel was saved from lion's den and the heated furnace by the Lord (Dan 3, 6). The high priests and all those who were with him called the council, all the senate of the people of Israel, and brought the disciples to the council again. Their issue was that the disciples taught the people at the temple and filled Jerusalem with their teachings (Acts 5:25, 28). According to this record, we can deduce how did the disciples' ministry of word strongly worked in Jerusalem and the cities around. However, though the religious leaders wanted to kill them, Gamaliel, a teacher of law who was respected by all the people, prohibited them not to touch them, so that they were released after being beaten and charged not to speak in the name of Jesus. However, the apostles, rejoicing that they were counted worthy to suffer dishonor for the name of Jesus, did not cease teaching and preaching that the Christ is Jesus, every day in the temple and from house to house (5:42). The disciples occupied the temple by teaching the word and they filled the whole city of Jerusalem with the word of God. The events of Ananias and Sapphira (5:1-11) and the choosing of the seven elders (6:1-17) show that the apostles devoted themselves completely to prayer and to the ministry of the word (6:4). Luke summarizes the apostles' ministry of Jerusalem by saying, "And the word of God continued to increase, and the number of the disciples multiplied greatly in Jerusalem, a great many of the priests became obedient to the faith" (6:7). The Holy Spirit at Pentecost came down to the city of Jerusalem and the ministry of the Spirit worked most powerfully and dynamically at Jerusalem in the history of Acts. However, Luke puts more emphasis on the apostles' ministry of the word than that of the Holy Spirit (Acts 2:42; 6:3–4).

The disciples' ministry of the word was not limited within Jerusalem and was not done by the apostles only. After Saul's persecution and following the death of Stephen (8:1–3), the disciples scattered to the areas of Judea and Samaria and witnessed to the events at Jerusalem and preached the word. Among them, Philip and Ananias's activities out of Jerusalem are noteworthy.

Philip at Judea and Samaria

The apostles' ministry of the word in Jerusalem was successful and the city seemed to be full of the word and the Spirit. It was almost like a scene that the prophecy of Isaiah was fulfilled and the peace was settled in it. However, the Lord no longer permitted this peace to be continued among them. The disciples were scattered to Judea and Samaria in order to escape Saul's persecution against the church in Jerusalem after Stephen's death (8:1). The disciples who left Jerusalem went about preaching the word. Therefore, the ministry of the word was expanded geographically from Jerusalem to Judea and Samaria, and through the ministers of the word, from the apostles to the deacons such as Stephen, Philip, Ananias, etc. Saul's persecution of the believers, particularly his stoning of Stephen, brought a turning point to the progress of the history of the apostle's ministry of the word.

Philip went to the city of Samaria and proclaimed the good news about the kingdom of God and the name of Jesus Christ. And he did miracles and cast out unclean spirits and healed the paralyzed and lame. His signs and deeds drew the attention of the crowd to him and led to their belief. Thus, Philip baptized them. Philip's ministry of the word among the Samaritans seems to be perfect; even Simon, who was regarded as a divine being by the all people of Samaria because of his powerful magic, believed and was baptized with all the people in the city. However, he lost his leadership and became one of the followers of Philip. If he could find any opportunity, he must surely have wanted to return his position of power. As it were, he was a latent threat to Philip in the Samaritan church. In those circumstances, Peter and John came to Samaria to pray for them and lay their hands on them, and they received the Holy Spirit (Acts 8:14–17). Since the Samaritans were baptized by Philip in the name of the Lord Jesus before the apostles arrived in Samaria, they did not need to be baptized by the Holy Spirit for their regeneration or their appointment to be the prophets. In this case, the coming of the Holy Spirit seems to be not for the Samaritans, but for the apostles and Philip in order to identify and witness them to be the servants of God.

First of all, the coming of the Holy Spirit was for Peter and John. The apostles demonstrated their authority with greater power than that of Philip. By this Peter and John condemned Simon's attempt to buy the Holy Spirit with money and discouraged his hidden desire to return his leadership from Philip. Through this series of events, Peter and John removed the possible danger of confusion in the church and firmly established order in the Samaritan church. Secondly, the coming of the Spirit to the Samaritan was for Philip. Through this miraculous event, Philip might have been recognized as God's servant and his works among them were also approved by God and eventually by the people as the work of God, not of man. Accordingly, the event of Samaria was not an extension of Pentecost, nor a "Samaritan Pentecost."[5]

By this Philip opened the door of the word to the Samaritans and even to the Ethiopian. The angel of the Lord instructed Philip

---

5. MacArthur asserts that "this was not a 'Samaritan Pentecost' but a crucial step of growth for church. There was only one Pentecost, and this added nothing to that. But it served as an audio-visual lesion to the whole church that the middle wall partition had indeed broken down." *Charismatic Chaos*, 182. Cf. Unger, *New Testament Teaching*, 36–37.

to meet the Ethiopian eunuch, and he explained the good news about Jesus from the book of Isaiah and baptized him with water, because the foreigner asked for it. However, when he came out of the water after baptism, the Spirit of the Lord carried Philip away, so that the Ethiopian could see him no more. This event might have given the conviction to the Ethiopian that he experienced the hand of saving grace of the Lord through the word.

Even though Philip was not an apostle, he was one of the disciples who was baptized by the Holy Spirit and chosen to serve at the table, and he was very actively involved in preaching the word of God. God did not distinguish between the apostles and the disciples in their prophetic ministry of the word.[6]

Ananias at Damascus

Ananias, a disciple at Damascus, a devout man according to the law and well spoken of by all the Jews who lived there, was called to help Saul, the persecutor of the saints in Jerusalem, to restore his sight and be baptized. He was not a refugee who fled to Damascus in order to escape from Saul's attack on the Christians in Jerusalem. The Lord himself appeared to Ananias in a vision and commanded him to go to Saul and lay his hands on him in order that he might receive his sight. But Ananias protested against the Lord's command, since he already had information about Saul's evil deeds and his purpose of coming to Damascus with the authority to arrest all who called on the name of Jesus. The Lord, then, revealed Saul's future role as "his chosen instrument" for

---

6. Considerable discussions have been raised on the absence of the Holy Spirit in Philip's ministry. Many scholars regard the appearance of the Spirit as a necessary sign of divine sanction of the ministry from God as well as the apostles of Jerusalem church. Keener, *Acts*, 2:1522. However, Calvin attested that the Samaritans were baptized because they were already received the Holy Spirit. Therefore, the purpose of Peter's laying hands on them was not for "general grace" (*communis spiritus gratia*) of their regeneration and speaking in tongues, but for "special gift" (*singularia dona*) in order for decoration of Christ's kingdom at the beginning of gospel. Calvin, *Acts*, on 8:16 (CR.76. ent 182).

the Gentiles (Acts 9:15–16). Ananias accepted his mission from the Lord and went to Saul and laid his hands on him. And he explained the purpose of his laying hands on him: "Brother Saul, the Lord Jesus who appeared to you on the road by which you came has sent me so that you may regain your sight and be filled with the Holy Spirit" (Acts 9:17). Immediately Saul regained his sight and was baptized. Actually, by this baptism he was installed as a new covenant prophet and a vessel for the Gentiles. Saul was given the special mission by the Lord through Ananias at the time of his baptism. He was chosen to be his instrument to carry his name for the Gentiles and kings and the children of Israel.[7] The Lord gave to Saul the special designation for his mission as "the vessel to carry the name of the Lord" (*tou bastasai to onoma mou*), which represents similar mission given to the other apostles.[8] Saul was given the gift of the Holy Spirit.[9]

Immediately after his baptism, Saul proclaimed Jesus in the synagogues, saying, "He is the Son of God" (9:20). As we observe this narrative of Saul's calling, the role of Ananias is very similar to that of prophets in the Old Testament when we were called and committed a certain mission. Ananias's mission was to appoint and install Saul as the chosen instrument of the Lord. He was not an apostle. He did not experience the baptism of the Holy Spirit at Pentecost. But he must have been baptized and became a member of the congregation at Damascus and had communion with the refugees from Jerusalem. However, he was called to play a

---

7. Kim with Betz explain Paul's call as the apostle for the Gentiles from his Damascus experience in view of Isaiah's call narrative in Old Testament (Isa 6). According to him, there are parallel points between Isaiah's call narrative and the Paul's Damascus event and Isa 49:5 is used for the background of Paul's understanding his mission as the apostle for the Gentiles in Rom 11:29f. *Origin*, 91–99.

8. The similar phrase "[my people] who are called by my name" (*'ammî ᵃšer niqrā šᵉmî*) in the Old Testament (Deut 28:10; 2 Chr 7:14; Isa 44:5; Jer 14:9, etc.) is a typical election phrase in the Old Testament used for a father-son relationship. Israel was chosen to be a name bearer of YHWH. Likewise, Saul was specially chosen to take the name of Christ throughout the world. Sohn, *Divine Election*, 69.

9. Cf. Barrett, *Acts*, 1:457.

The Activities of the New Covenant Prophets

prophetical role to install Saul to be the "chosen instrument" of the Lord. This reminds us of the relationship between Samuel and Saul in the Old Testament. As Samuel anointed Saul, the son of Kish, to be the king of Israel, Ananias baptized Saul, the persecutor, by laying his hands on him to be the "chosen instrument to carry the name of the Lord before the gentiles and kings and the children of Israel." This story of Ananias shows that Saul did not speak in tongues when he was baptized, but he experienced the miracle of loosing and gaining his sight. This may have given him a strong confidence that God called him as a new covenant prophet.

Luke reports the apostles' ministry of the word as follows: "So the church throughout all Judea and Galilee and Samaria had peace and was being built up. And walking in the fear of the Lord and in the comfort of the Holy Spirit, it multiplied" (Acts 9:31). The ministry of the word expanded geographically from Jerusalem to the regions of Judea, Galilee, and Samaria, and personally from the apostles to Philip, Ananias, Barnabas, and even to Saul, who was a persecutor of the church and took the initiative to stone Stephen to death. Wherever they proclaimed the word of God, there arose dynamic activities of the Holy Spirit together.

To the End of the Earth

The disciples' ministry of the word after the baptism of the Holy Spirit at Pentecost was heading for Rome, the end of the earth. It crossed the border of Judea and Samaria and arrived in Antioch, and Paul was a main character from there on, mainly among the Gentiles.

Antioch

Antioch was a central church for Paul's ministry of the word to Rome. Barnabas, who was sent from Jerusalem and felt the need for a Bible teacher there, went to Tarsus to invite him. He was ostracized by the people because of his persecution against the church and stayed at his home. However, the members of the Antioch church mostly heard the witnesses of the scattered because of his persecution against the disciples at Jerusalem. Barnabas and Saul preached to them and taught them and a great many people joined to them, and there they were first called "Christians" (11:26). In the church of Antioch there were prophets and teachers, such as Barnabas, Simon, Lucius, Manaen, and Saul (13:1).[10] This shows that the main activity of the disciples in the church of Antioch was teaching the word of God. God commanded to set apart Barnabas and Saul for the work of the word to the nations. According to this command, Saul and Barnabas began their missionary journey throughout the world, eventually to Rome.

Ephesus

Ephesus was a strategic city for Paul in his missionary project to go to Rome. After the end of his second missionary journey, he visited Ephesus to decide his destination for his third journey on his way back to Jerusalem and Antioch. He met Jews in the synagogue and reasoned with them and he seemed to make a decision to come back if possible (Acts 18:18–21). Before Paul arrived in Ephesus there were some disciples who had already been taught by Apollos, who was eloquent and competent in the Scriptures, and by the couple of Priscilla and Aquila, who were tentmakers by trade with Paul at Corinth. As he began his ministry of the word, Paul needed to make his identity known to them. When he recognized their ignorance about the Holy Spirit, he laid his hands on them. Then the Holy Spirit came down and the twelve of them spoke in tongues and prophesied. They were already believers in

---

10. During the reign of Jehoshaphat, the king of Judah, he sent his officials, Levites, and priests to teach in the cities of Judah, having the book of the Lord with them. This brought to Judah religious, economic, and military strength and power. We can find this similar name list of teaching the law in Neh 8:7–9. The Chronicler's intention of recording the names participated in the ministry of the word of God seems to show the importance of the word in the redemptive history.

The Activities of the New Covenant Prophets

Jesus,[11] thus we cannot say that they received the Holy Spirit for their regeneration and their salvation. It was primarily to testify Paul as "the man of God" who was different from their teachers in Ephesus. Another purpose in his laying on of hands was to appoint them to be the new covenant prophets who could work with him, because they spoke in tongues as well as prophesied when the Holy Spirit came on them.[12] When the twelve of them recognized the identity of Paul and of themselves, they followed Paul to the synagogue and to the hall of Tyrannus to evangelize the whole city of Ephesus and Asia. When the event of the seven sons of a Jewish priest became known to all the residents of Ephesus, fear fell upon them and the name of the Lord Jesus was extolled. Luke continues his report:

> Also many of those who were now believers come, confessing and divulging their practices. And a number of those who had practiced magic are brought their books together and burned them in the sight of all. And they counted the value of them and found it came to fifty thousand pieces of silver. So the word of the Lord continued to increase and prevail mightily. (Acts 19:18–20)

---

11. Some scholars assert that they are not to be called Christians because they were not baptized by the name of the Lord Jesus. However, as Barrett says, it is natural to regard Apollos as a Christian because he was instructed in the way of the Lord. Luke is referring "the way" to Christianity and "the Lord" to Jesus. And in Acts 18:25, Luke is introducing him as "Being fervent in spirit, he spoke and taught accurately the things concerning Jesus." And further, we can see that Paul regarded them as believers in 19:1–2. He called the Ephesians as "disciples" and asked, "Did you received the Holy Spirit when you believed?" Barrett, *Acts*, 2:885–87. Lange, et al., *Acts*, 348–49. For the negative discussions on this subject, please refer to Keener, *Acts*, 15:1–23:35, 3:2814–20. Apollos was taught by Priscilla and Aquila about the way of God more accurately and left Ephesus for Achaia before Paul's arrival at Ephesus. When he (Apollo) arrived Achaia, "he greatly helped those who through grace had believed, for he powerfully refuted the Jews in public, showing by the Scriptures that the Christ was Jesus" (Acts 18:27–28).

12. For more explanation, see the section in chapter 6 entitled "Paul and the Ephesian Disciples."

The expansion of the word was brought by Paul and his twelve prophet-disciples by their teaching in the hall of Tyrannus. Paul's ministry of disciple-making was successful. However, this event influenced the idol sellers in the market and brought a riot against Paul. He had to leave the city and said, "I must also see Rome." His next destination was confirmed at the event of the riot.

Rome

As he left Ephesus, Paul resolved in the Spirit to return to Jerusalem. And he said, "After I have been there, I must also see Rome" (19:21). Afterward, he arrived in Rome in chains as the prisoner of the emperor and stayed at an inn. He began his ministry of the word there.

> When they appointed a day for him, they came to him at his lodging in great numbers. From morning till evening, he expounded to them, testifying to the kingdom of God and trying to convince them about Jesus both from the Law of Moses and from the prophet. (Acts 28:23)

Later, he moved his dwelling place. "He lived there two whole years at his own expense, and welcomed all who came to him, proclaiming the kingdom of God and teaching about the Lord Jesus Christ with all boldness and without hindrance" (Acts 28:30). As the Lord Jesus commanded his disciples before his ascension to go to the ends of the earth, Paul came to Rome and taught about Jesus Christ to the people there.

Acts is a history about the disciple's activities from Jerusalem to Rome after the baptism of the Holy Spirit at Pentecost. Luke, in his writing, inserted signposts that inform about the progress of the word at the significant turning points from Jerusalem to Rome.

When the disciples' ministry moved from Jerusalem to Judea and Samaria, he writes, "The word of God continued to increase, and member of the disciples multiplied greatly in Jerusalem and a great many of the priest become obedient to the faith" (Acts 6:7). At the end of ministry in Judea and Samaria, Luke writes,

The Activities of the New Covenant Prophets

> So the church throughout all Judea and Galilee and Samaria had peace and was being built up. And walking in the fear of the Lord and in the comfort of the Holy Spirit, it multiplied. (9:31)

> But the word of God increased and multiplied. (12:24)

Luke emphasizes that the ministry of the world evangelization begun in Antioch was a result of the ministry of the word through the prophets and teachers.

> And when the Gentiles heard this, they began rejoicing and glorifying the word of the Lord, and as many as were appointed to eternal life believed. And the word of the Lord was spreading throughout the whole region. (13:48–49)

> But Paul and Barnabas remained in Antioch, teaching and preaching the word of the Lord, with many others also. (15:35)

Luke continually focuses his concern on the ministry of the word in Ephesus and Rome (Acts 19:20; 28: 23). Finally, he concluded the book of Acts with the scene of Paul teaching the word in his hired house.[13]

As we observed above, Luke writes about the progress of the disciples' ministry of the word: how it begin from Jerusalem and reached to Rome. In his narrative he inserted the phrase "so the word of the Lord continued to increase and prevail mightily" as a key to guide his readers to where the flow of the ministry of the word was heading and to show the work of the word and the disciples as the new covenant prophets, the servants of the word.

However, Deasley affirms that Luke's primary concern in Acts is "with the Spirit as the agent of mission; hence the emphatic insistence at each of the nodal points in the advance of the gospel that spirit is poured out. His basic intent is to show that the Christian era is the era of the Spirit; that there is no Church without the

---

13. Kistemaker and Hendriksen, *Exposition*, 447.

Spirit; no Christian without the Spirit and wherever the gospel goes in power, it goes in the power of the Spirit."[14] On this affirmation, we cannot but point out that he overlooks that Luke's intention was to emphasize the role of the word more than the Spirit in the progress of the gospel to Rome. Acts is the book about how Jesus' disciples proclaimed the teachings of their Lord from Jerusalem to Rome as he commanded them. Therefore, wherever the ministry of the word worked actively and mightily, he commented, "So the word of the Lord continued to increase and prevail mightily." It is good for Deasley to emphasize the role of the Spirit, but Acts is a book about the word, a history of how the disciples preached the word of God as the Lord had commanded them. The word and the Spirit are inseparable. Where the word is preached, the Spirit works, and the Spirit works with the word. Even though the Spirit takes the initiative in the ministry, it works where the word is proclaimed and preached by the disciples, who were installed as the new covenant prophets by the baptism of the Spirit at Pentecost.

Jesus appointed his disciples and gave the baptism of the Holy Spirit for the purpose of the ministry of the word. The baptism of the Holy Spirit was the installing and sealing ceremony of the disciples as the new covenant prophets to work for the global ministry of the word. Accordingly, it was needed for those who work for the ministry of the word, and it was not to be repeated since it was an installation ceremony for the prophetic calling. Thus, it is not correct to insist that the baptism of the Holy Spirit at Pentecost should be repeated, because the people spoke in tongues when the apostles preached the word of God and laid their hands on them. Gaffin is correct when he calls the Holy Spirit the universal Spirit, because the unprecedented worldwide ministry of the word had been brought about after the baptism of the Holy Spirit at Pentecost,[15] but it is not persuasive to say that we should not emphasize the Holy Spirit at Pentecost as the Spirit of mission. Furthermore, it is not satisfactory enough to explain the uniqueness of the baptism with the Holy Spirit at Pentecost on the

14. Deasley, "Entire Sanctification," 1.
15. Gaffin, "Holy Spirit," 73.

The Activities of the New Covenant Prophets

basis that the ministry of the word of Philip at Samaria, of Peter at Cornelius's house, and of Paul at Ephesus are the extension or continuation of the event at Pentecost. The baptism of the Holy Spirit was the installation ceremony of Jesus' disciples as the new covenant prophets. That is why it is not repeatable.[16]

After Rome, the disciples began to write the word of God that was committed to them, and they left the scrolls and epistles as the Old Testamant prophets did. Obviously, the disciples of Jesus succeeded the prophetic ministry of the word in the Old Testament and they were to make disciples after them to proclaim it through the Bible to all nations until the end of the age.

---

16. Gaffin, *Perpectives*, 22.

6

The Related Themes and Their Applications

A new interpretation of the event of Pentecost as an installation ceremony for the new covenant prophets on the basis of a literal translation has been proposed. If this interpretation is correct, the related theological subjects and their interpretations that have been retained until now need to be examined and corrected. New understandings, different roles, and proper applications of the baptism of the Holy Spirit are also required.

The Once-and-for-Allness of the Baptism of the Holy Spirit

If the baptism of the Holy Spirit was an installation ceremony for the disciples in their role as new covenant prophets, then it is an event that is not to be repeated. This is not an unusual case. A variety of installation ceremonies are performed only once, never to be repeated.[1] No further explanation for this is necessary. As has been noted earlier, the phrase "to be baptized by the Holy Spirit" is

---

1. Unger writes, "It is unrepeatable as the creation of the universe, the creation of man, the incarnation of Christ, His sinless life, vicarious death, glorious resurrection, or any other event of history." *Baptism and Gifts*, 62.

The Related Themes and Their Applications

limited in its usage in the Bible. However, Ryon, a Wesleyan Theologian, affirms:

> From the Pentecost on, all the believers received at conversion the Holy Spirit as promised—in his fullness. No biblical basis exists for a distinction between receiving the Spirit and being baptized in, or filled with the Spirit. The Acts of the Apostles shows *au contraire* that they are interchangeable expressions. All references involving the language of baptism reinforce that conclusion, for they are all inclusive as a descriptive of every believer.[2]

But the phrases "reception of the Holy Spirit," "baptism of the Holy Spirit," and "the fullness of the Holy Spirit" are not used interchangeably in the Bible. In fact, the term "baptism of the Holy Spirit" is used only twice in the Bible.[3] The first occurrence appears when Jesus was baptized with water by John the Baptist, and it signified the inauguration of Jesus' messianic ministry. At that time, John introduced Jesus as the one who would baptize with the Holy Spirit and fire (Luke 3:16). Many people regard this verse as a reference to the event of Pentecost. However, there was no fire at Pentecost. There were divided tongues descending from above, and these were seen as a divided flame of fire. The fire mentioned by John should rather be understood as describing Jesus as the Lord of judgment, since fire usually symbolizes the judgment of the last days.[4] When Jesus was baptized by water, the Holy Spirit descended on him in bodily form, like a dove, and a voice came from heaven saying, "You are my beloved Son; with you I am well pleased" (Luke 3:22). Thus, as Jesus began his ministry of the word, he was installed as the Great Prophet by the Holy Spirit.[5] God announced the beginning of his Son's messianic ministry through the baptism of the Holy Spirit.

The second case is related to the event of Pentecost, to the disciples, who were about to begin the ministry of prophet. When

2. Quoted in Hart, "Spirit Baptism," 213.
3. Elwell, *Evangelical Commentary*, vol. 3, on Acts 2:2–13.
4. Marshall, *Luke*, 145–49.
5. Marshall, *Luke*, 154.

His Touch on the Mouths

Jesus rose from the dead and met his disciples in Jerusalem, he commanded them not to leave from there and instructed them "to wait for the promise of the Father," because they would be "baptized with the Holy Spirit" not many days from then (Acts 1:4–5). Just as Jesus began his ministry of the word by receiving the baptism of the Holy Spirit, so would the disciples begin their ministry of the word as new covenant prophets when they were baptized with the Holy Spirit. Therefore, this event of baptism is not an event to be repeated.

However, most Pentecostals regard speaking in tongues as the initial physical evidence of the baptism of the Holy Spirit. Charismatics take a softer position and say that though they can or not speak in tongues, speaking in tongues is possible for all people, and affirm that it is a part of normal Christian life with the fullness of the Spirit.[6] Finney, a charismatic, believed in repeated baptisms in the Spirit as a normal part of the Christian life and he himself experienced several such baptisms.[7] Jones writes on the repetition of the baptism of the Holy Spirit as follows:

> Examine your doctrine of the Holy Spirit, and in the name of God, be careful lest, in your neat and trimmed doctrine, you are excluding and putting out this most remarkable thing which God does periodically through the Holy Spirit, in sending him upon us, in visiting, in baptizing us, in reviving the whole church in a miraculous and astonishing manner.
>
> Do you believe in revival, my friend? Are you praying for revival? What are you trusting? Or are you trusting in the power of God to pour out his Spirit upon us again, to revive us, to baptize us anew and afresh with his most blessed Holy Spirit? The church needs another Pentecost. Every revival is a repetition of Pentecost, and it is the greatest need of the Christian church at this present hour.[8]

---

6. Hart, "Spirit Baptism," 123.

7. Gresham, *Charles G. Finney's Doctrine*, 86, quoted in Brand, ed., *Perspectives*, 227.

8. Lloyd-Jones, *Unspeakable Power*, 280.

The Related Themes and Their Applications

Jones attests that believers need the repeated baptism of the Holy Spirit for an energetic and dynamic Christian life. Every revival, he believes, followed by the repetition of Pentecost.

On this issue, Kuyper provides a graphic analogy to illustrate the continuity of the baptism of the Holy Spirit at Pentecost and the events that follow by comparing the water system of two parts of a city. Following is a quotation from his explanation on this issue.

> Suppose that a city whose citizens for ages have been drinking each from his own cistern proposes to construct a reservoir that will supply every home. When the work is completed the water is allowed to run through the system of mains and pipes into every house . . .
>
> Suppose that the city above referred to consisted of a lower and upper part, both to be supplied by the same reservoir . . . the distribution of the water took place but once, which was the formal opening of the water works, and could take place but once; while the distribution of the water in the upper city, although extraordinary, was but an after-effect of the former event . . . on Pentecost He [*i.e.* the Spirit] is poured out into the body, but only to quench the thirst of one, *i.e.* the Jewish . . . hence there is an *original* outpouring in Jerusalem on the day of Pentecost, and a *supplementary* outpouring in Caesarea for the gentile part of the Church: both of the same nature, but each bearing its own special character.
>
> Besides these there are some isolated outpouring of the Holy Spirit, attended by laying one of the apostles' hands . . . from time to time new connections are made between individual houses and the city reservoir, so new parts of the body of Christ were added to the church from without, into whom the Holy Spirit was poured forth from the body as into new members . . .[9]

According to him the Pentecost and the events that followed it are of same in nature, but each bearing its own character. And the outpouring of the Holy Spirit in Jerusalem was *original*, like a reservoir of an old city that was filled with water at one time. And the following events at Samaria and Ephesus for the Gentiles were

9. Kuyper, *Work*, 123–26, quoted in Ferguson, *Holy Spirit*, 85–86.

supplementary and were distributed through the pipes connected to the *original*.

Therefore, Kuyper's explanation in the analogy of a water system in the two parts of a city leads us to think that there were two Pentecosts, two baptisms, same in nature but different in character. However, there is no such concept in the Bible of dividing the baptism into two parts, original and supplementary. There was only one perfect and full baptism of the Holy Spirit at Pentecost. There were no more such things similar to Pentecost. The other events in the early churches were entirely different in nature and character. Though Kuyper seems to explain the once-for-allness of the baptism of the Holy Spirit, he overlooks the nature and function of it as the installation of the disciples as the new covenant prophets. Since it is installation ceremony, it is not to be repeated. It is a ceremony to testify the disciples as the prophets of God and to bestow on them authority and power for the prophetic ministry of the word.

However, as we have surveyed, there are many who assert that the baptism of the Spirit should be repeated on the basis of a so-called "Johannine Pentecost" and the phenomena of speaking in tongues among the Cornelius household and Ephesian disciples. And even though there are those who maintain the once-for-allness of the baptism of the Holy Spirit, their theological basis for their attestations are not satisfactory. But a closer examination of those events will reveal that they do not support their assertions.

"Johannine Pentecost"

John 20:19–20 is known as the "Johannine Pentecost" among those who assert the repetition of the baptism of the Holy Spirit at Pentecost, because the narrative is almost similar to that of the baptism of the Holy Spirit at Pentecost in Acts. However, a closer examination shows that it is entirely different story. Before we proceed to examine the texts in order to find the proper interpretation, it would be natural to survey the different proposals raised

The Related Themes and Their Applications

on the repetition of the baptism of the Holy Spirit, including the "Johannine Pentecost." Four views seem to be circulated.

First of all, two Pentecost theories. Most Pentecostals, charismatics, and Wesleyans follow this interpretation. According to them, the "Johannine Pentecost" and Lukan Pentecost are essentially same, but they took place in a different time and place. This means that the baptism of the Holy Spirit should be repeated. However, Ladd rightly points out the problem with this as follows: "It is difficult to believe there were two impartations of the Spirit. The Fourth Gospel itself teaches that the Spirit could not be given until Jesus' ascension, and so if this is the actual bestowment, there would need to be two ascensions. However, there is no evidence that the disciples began to carry out their mission until after Pentecost."[10] In the Johannine record there is no voice of a mighty rushing wind, no divided tongues like fire from above, no disciples speaking in tongues, and no response from the people. There was only one word of describing Jesus' breathing on them and commanding them to receive the Holy Spirit. It is hard to find any decisive evidence for the similarity between the two.

Second, a typological interpretation. Ladd regards Luke's narrative and "John's Pentecost" as essentially same and suggests that this "inbreathing" was an acted parable promissory and anticipatory to the actual coming of the Spirit at Pentecost.[11] For him the "Johannine Pentecost" is a type of Lukan Pentecost in Acts. And someone has noticed that the Greek word *empysaō* ("to breath") in the Greek versions was translated from the Hebrew word *napaḥ*. They draw an analogy from this usage of the word: as this word was used in God's breathing of life into the nostrils of Adam (Gen 2:7) and into the dry bones of the slain in the valley of vision (Ezek 37:1–14), Jesus now breathed his new life into his disciples. Therefore, the action of Jesus' breathing in John primarily represents the impartation of the life that the Holy Spirit gives in the new age, brought about through Christ's exaltation in death and resurrection. They regard this as the beginning of the new creation and

10. Dunning, "Wesleyan Perspective," 225.
11. Ibid.

new age.¹² However, it is hard to say that "Johannine Pentecost" and Luke's record concerning the resurrection of Jesus and following the baptism of the Holy Spirit at Pentecost constitute a type and antitype relationship. They are entirely different events.

Third, the "John's Pentecost" as a foretaste of Lukan Pentecost. Beasley-Murray introduces a few illustrations for this view:

> Likewise it is inadequate to view the gift of Christ as a *partial* bestowal of the Spirit who is to be *fully* given at Pentecost, an idea expressed in a variety of ways. Calvin considered "the Spirit was given to the apostles now in such a way that they were only *sprinkled* with his grace and not *saturated* with full power" (*Gospel according to St. John*, 11–21 [Edinburgh: Oliver and Boyd, 1961] 205, cited by Turner, "Receiving the Spirit in John's Gospel," 32). Bengel viewed the gift as an "earnest" of Pentecost, Westcott as *the power of new life* anticipating the *power for ministry* (350–51); Bruce inverts the order, seeing the Easter gift as *empowerment for ministry*, to be followed by the Spirit's *gift of new life* at Pentecost.¹³

This theory basically presupposes the double Pentecost. For them the first one (Johannine) is the foretaste and the second one (Pentecost) is the full and perfect one. However, the so-called "Johannine Pentecost," according to our understanding, was not the baptism of the Holy Spirit. There is no similarity in its basic nature with the Pentecost event.

Fourth, the view that they are the same event but two different perspectives and descriptions. According to Beasley-Murray, John views the resurrection, the baptism of the Holy Spirit, and the ascension of Jesus as unified event and he does not write of those events according to chronology. This means the baptism of the Holy Spirit could have been at any time within the Easter period. However, Luke binds the baptism of the Holy Spirit to the resurrection of Jesus. Beasley-Murray concludes on this issue as follows:

---

12. Beasley-Murray, *John*, 381.
13. Ibid.

The Related Themes and Their Applications

What, then, is our conclusion? The Fourth Evangelist does not specify the Easter events according to chronology. He could perfectly well have been aware of the Pentecostal tradition and write exactly as he has done. But there is no question of viewing the sending of the Spirit as taking place at Easter and at Pentecost. It is one or the other, in view of the nature of each Evangelist's presentation of the event. In the judgment of the present writer, the Lukan narrative in Acts 2 is an authentic account of the coming of the Spirit at the celebration of the giving of the Law, when the company of the new covenant received power to proclaim the message of the new covenant in tongues for the whole world to hear, just as the word of the old covenant was so proclaimed amidst flames of fire (the narrative is shot through with the symbolism of the festival, just as John 7–8 reflects the celebration of Tabernacles; see J. H. E. Hull, *The Holy Spirit in the Acts of the Apostles*, 48–56). The Fourth Evangelist wrote one volume only, not two, as Luke. What he wrote concerning the coming of the Spirit was theologically and historically sound, as, I am persuaded, was that written by his brother in the Lord, Luke.[14]

This view of Beasley-Murray seems to be quite possible. Borchert agrees with him that there is only one giving of the Spirit and it can be described from various points of view. From this presupposition he extends the meaning of the event. He views this event as the defense of the son's role in the coming of the Spirit against any reduction of Jesus' divine nature. He asserts that John intended to show that it is Jesus, indeed, in union with God, who has sent the Spirit (John 15:20).[15] However, these scholars disregard the continuity of Jesus' disciples with the prophets in the Old Testament. The baptism of the Holy Spirit at Pentecost was God's installation ceremony for Jesus' disciples to be his new covenant prophets for the work of the word in redeeming the world by his word.

---

14. Ibid., 382.
15. Borchert, *John 12–21*, 309.

His Touch on the Mouths

As we have considered the above interpretations, a more careful and precise exposition for the narrative in John seems to be required. When Jesus came to his disciples, they have themselves locked in a room for fear of the Jews. The sudden presence of the risen Jesus among them could have increased their fear. Jesus bid them peace and showed them his hands and side, then (*oun*) they were glad to see him. And in verse 21 Jesus bids peace again. Here John uses the word "again" (*palin*), which is reflection of the disciples' mind of fear. Then he revealed the purpose of his return to them, saying, "As the father has sent me, even so I am sending you." He is saying that he was sent by the Father, so his return is not his own will, but the Father's will. He seems to play the role of messenger or prophet of the Father in the Old Testament. "And when he said this, and breathed on them and said to them, 'Receive the Holy Spirit" (*kai touto eipōn evepysēsen kai legei autois. lambete pneuma hagion*). The abnormal tense of the verbs is noticeable here in the Greek version, but most of English versions disregard this and emend it to make it readable. Since the Greek *'enephysēsen* (ἐνεφύσησεν, "breathed," aor. ind.) is in the aorist tense and the next verb, *légei* (λέγει, say. pres. ind.), is in the present tense, the normal translation should be "and saying this, he breathed and says to them, 'Receive Holy Spirit,'" as in the German version of ELB6. Whatever the translation might be, the fact that John uses the tense of verbs differently is important. John makes a time brake between these two actions of Jesus. Jesus breathed and paused a little bit and began to say to receive the Spirit. So, we can say that John inserted an intentional time gap or change in order to show that Jesus' breathing and commandment to receive the Spirit are not continuous and simultaneous actions. In another words, the two actions have nothing to do with each other. Furthermore, those on whom Jesus breathed is not specified in the Greek text. But the English versions add "on them" and mislead their readers to understand as if Jesus breathed something into the nose of his disciples.

Then why did Jesus breathe here? Those who propose a typological interpretation relate the Greek word *empysaō* with the

The Related Themes and Their Applications

Hebrew word *nāpaḥ*. As this word was used for God's breathing of life into the nostrils of Adam (Gen 2:7) and into the dry bones of the slain in the valley of vision (Ezek 37:1–14), they apply God's breathing into Adam to Jesus' breathing into his disciples at the "Johannine Pentecost." However, the object of God's breathing is clearly specified in Gen 2:7. It was the "*nišmat ḥayyim*", translated usually as the "breath of life." As God breathed *nišmat ḥayyim* into his nostrils and the man became a *nepeš ḥayyah* ("living creature"), the risen Jesus breathed his new life into his disciples to be new men and to open a new world. However, John 20:22 does not use *ruaḥ*, a general term for Spirit, nor the technical term *nišmat ḥayyim*, and does not specify the object of the verb. John seems to be fully aware of this and does not use "*ho*" (ό), the definite article before "Holy Spirit" (*pneuma hagion*) in the context.[16] A dead body is generally discerned by checking for breath. Therefore, we can safely say that Jesus' breathing in John 22:19–23 has nothing to do with the baptism of the Holy Spirit at Pentecost. Jesus is just breathing as ordinary man. He is showing that he has been raised and now is alive as an ordinary man. Jesus is demonstrating to his disciples that he is alive, and so he calms down the minds of the disciples, who are in fear of Jews and even Jesus himself. The commandment to receive the Holy Spirit is his guidance for the following events. They will be baptized to be the prophets of God and preach the gospel of the forgiveness of sins. Therefore, the so-called "Johannine Pentecost" does not exist.

If Jesus had breathed the Holy Spirit into his disciples and they became new men, as interpreters assert, they would not have locked themselves in the house after eight days and Jesus would not have said again, "Peace be with you." The fear of the Jews remained still in their mind. Thus, Jesus told Thomas to look at his hands and put his finger into his side and said, "Do not disbelieve, but believe . . . Blessed are those who have not seen and yet have believed" (20:27–29). And Thomas confessed, "My Lord, My God." However, in John 21 the disciples come back to Galilee and

---

16. ibid, 380. However, many of the exegets and translators of this verse disregard this except for German Bible, BLB6.

become fishermen again. Nothing new happens to them after his meeting. The supposed Johannine Pentecost is full of the fear, despair, frustration, helplessness, and disbelief of the disciples. There is nothing like the baptism of the Holy Spirit at Pentecost. Nothing can be compared with Lukan narrative. The baptism of the Holy Spirit was not for salvation or sanctification. It was a ceremony for installing Jesus' disciples as the new covenant prophets. There is no need for it to be repeated.

Peter and the Household of Cornelius

Peter went to visit Cornelius's house as he had been instructed in a vision, preaching the word of God as his request. Even though Cornelius and his household did not clearly know the identity of Peter, they gathered around to hear him speak. And as Peter was talking, they spoke in tongues.

> While Peter was still saying these things, the Holy Spirit fell on all who heard the word. And the believers from among the circumcised who had come with Peter were amazed, because the gift of the Holy Spirit was poured out even on the Gentiles. For they were hearing them speaking in tongues and extolling God. (Acts 10:44–46)

Here, what amazed the circumcised was that the "the gift of the Holy Spirit" (*hē dōrea tou hagiou pneumatos*, 10:45) was given even to the Gentiles. What is to be noted at this point is that they were not "baptized by the Holy Spirit" (*en pneumati hagiō baptisthēsan*), but they were given "the gift of the Holy Spirit" (*hē dōrea tou hagiou pneumatos*). This is clearly different from the baptism of the Holy Spirit at Pentecost. Indeed, it is similar to Peter's reply to the three thousand whom he told to repent and be baptized in the name of Jesus in order to receive "the gift of the Holy Spirit" (2:38). One can hardly say that God sent Peter to Cornelius's household to appoint them to be prophets of God. Cornelius said to Peter, "We are all here in the presence of God to hear all that you have commanded by the Lord" (10:33). He acknowledged

The Related Themes and Their Applications

Peter as "the spokesman of God" who was there to deliver the word of God. Thus, Peter spoke the word of God to them as his prophet. At this moment, God sent the Holy Spirit, enabling them to speak in tongues in order that they might recognize Peter as a prophet, "the man of God." In this event, it is evident that the purpose of speaking in tongues is not for Cornelius's household, but rather for Peter's benefit. God acknowledged him as his prophet by sending the Holy Spirit while he was speaking, making it possible for those in Cornelius's household to speak in tongues so that they might receive what Peter said as the word of God.

Luke describes the result of this event after Peter returned to Jerusalem and reported what had transpired to the other disciples as follows: "Now the apostles and the brothers who were throughout Judea heard that the Gentiles also had received the word of God" (11:1). He does not mention anything about the Gentiles' speaking in tongues. Instead, he depicts the entire event as being the ministry of the word. In 11:16 Peter recalls the events at the house of Cornelius, saying, "And I remembered the word of the Lord, how he said, 'John baptized with water, but you will be baptized with the Holy Spirit.'" Peter, remembering the words of the risen Jesus, is assured that he is a prophet of the Lord by receiving the baptism of the Holy Spirit, and he commanded them with conviction to be baptized in the name of Jesus. This episode is very similar to the event at Jerusalem when Peter delivered the self-justifying speech in which he asked his listeners to be baptized in the name of Jesus Christ (2:38).

When Peter commanded the household of Cornelius to be baptized, he asked, "Can anyone withhold water for baptizing these people, who have received the Holy Spirit just as we have?" (10:47). But when he returned to Jerusalem and reported what had taken place at Cornelius's house, he responded to his critics, "If then God gave the same gift to them as he gave to us when we believed in the Lord Jesus Christ, who was I that I could stand in God's way?" (*ei oun tēn isaēn dōrean edōken autois ho theos hōs kai hemin pisteusasin epi ton kyrion Iēsoun Christon, egō tis ēmēn dynatos kōlusai ton theon*, 11:17).[17] Peter added the phrase "when we believed in the Lord Jesus Christ." This addition obviously implies the intended theological meaning of 10:44. Furthermore, in 11:15 Peter states, "As I began to speak, the Holy Spirit fell on them just as on us at the beginning." What event was he referring to as having occurred "at the beginning"? If viewed in connection with verse 17, it appears that Peter is not referring to the time of the baptism of the Holy Spirit at Pentecost. Rather, he seems to be referencing the time when they first believed in Jesus, and the gift of the Holy Spirit that first worked in them to cause them to believe. Therefore, Peter clearly distinguished between the baptism of the Holy Spirit that occurred at Pentecost in Jerusalem, which served to acknowledge the disciples as prophets of the new covenant, and the gift of the Holy Spirit that Cornelius and his household received when they believed in Jesus. For Cornelius and his household, the gift of the Holy Spirit marked the inception of their faith through the regeneration of the Holy Spirit, as Dunn has said.[18]

Therefore, it is evident that there were two purposes for the event of their speaking in tongues in Cornelius's home. The first was for Peter. God gave them the Holy Spirit in order that they might speak in tongues and recognize that Peter was a man of God sent by him. Even though Peter does not say that this is the baptism of the Holy Spirit, he recognizes that it plays the role of awakening his prophetic mission.

The second purpose was for Cornelius's household. The Holy Spirit had awakened the people of Cornelius by letting them speak in tongues in order to recognize that mysterious things were working in themselves. However, we cannot say that this is the baptism

---

17. This verse has been translated numerous ways: "... gave the same gift to them as he gave to us when we believed in the Lord Jesus Christ" (ESV), "... gave us after we believed..." (NASB, NET), "... gave us who believed..." (NIV), "... gave them when they believed the same gift as he also gave us..." (NRS). However, if v. 15 refers to the baptism of the Holy Spirit (ἐν δὲ τῷ ἄρξασθαί με λαλεῖν ἐπέπεσεν τὸ πνεῦμα τὸ ἅγιον ἐπ' αὐτοὺς ὥσπερ καὶ ἐφ' ἡμᾶς ἐν ἀρχῇ, Acts 11:15) then v. 17 deals with the gift of the Holy Spirit, which is distinguished from the former.

18. Dunn, *Baptism*, 51.

The Related Themes and Their Applications

of the Holy Spirit, because Peter did not intend to appoint or install them to be prophets. It was the gift of the Holy Spirit for the believers. They received the gift of the Holy Spirit as salvation just as the apostles did when they first believed. Since Peter realized that the household of Cornelius received the same gift of the Spirit, the gift of regeneration when he first believed, he baptized them with water and accepted them as members of Christ.[19]

Thus, the incident of the baptism of the Holy Spirit at Cornelius's house should not be taken as proof of a repetitive nature of the baptism of the Holy Spirit. Peter realized that God had given the same gift of the Holy Spirit to the Gentiles, the uncircumcised, as he had given to the Jews, the circumcised. He understood that these Romans also became the people of God by receiving the word of God, the Holy Spirit, and baptism, just as the Jews had. Peter, who was baptized by the Holy Spirit, baptized these Gentiles with water, being accompanied by the gift of the Holy Spirit, and he ate and drank with them as they asked him to do. He accepted them as the people of God and as a clean people (10:48; 11:1–3).[20] Thus, the event had the historical significance of expanding what had been a Jewish-centered ministry to include the Gentiles as well. Peter became the first apostle to open the door of the word to the Gentiles.[21] In that sense, some view the event as a "Gentile Pentecost." Unger understands this event as the inaugural rite to open the door of the word to the Gentiles:

> At Caesarea as at Pentecost the sign of supernatural language (Acts 10:46) was connected with the inauguration of new age. Pentecost opened the inaugural phase. The event at Caesarea closed it and marked the attainment of normal course of the new era. The tongues were a witness to the Jews of this fact. Peter and the Jewish witnesses who accompanied him to Caesarea were fully assured by divine intervention that the new age had been

---

19. Calvin, in *CR* 26:51.
20. Barrett, *Acts*, 527–31.
21. MacArthur, *Charismatic Chaos*, 180–81. Polhill, *Acts*, 264.

fully introduced and its normal order set with the outgoing of gospel privilege to the Gentiles.[22]

Unger is quite right that he sees the event at Caesarea as an inaugural rite for the opening of new age and the supernatural language as the sign of testifying this fact to the people. However, he misses the point that speaking in tongues was primarily for the divine witness of Peter as the man of God, the new covenant prophet.

Therefore, it should be distinguished from the event of Pentecost that occurred in Jerusalem. The Jerusalem event, the baptism of the Holy Spirit, served the purpose of installing the disciples as new covenant prophets and bestowing them with the requisite power and authority to fulfill Jesus' mandate to make disciples of all nations. But the gift of the Holy Spirit that Cornelius and his household received served to make them believers and eventually afterward to be disciple makers.

Paul and the Ephesian Disciples

Paul had a long-term goal of going to Rome and beginning his ministry there. Thus, he chose Ephesus as a strategic place for his third missionary journey. At the end of his second missionary journey, he made an on-the-stop survey of Ephesus in order to prepare for the establishment of the strategic center for the evangelism of Rome. However, when he arrived at the city, there were many disciples who had already heard the gospel from competent teachers such as Apollos, Priscilla, and Aquila. Priscilla and Aquila practiced the same trade as Paul—tent making—and they had stayed with Paul at Corinth before they came to Ephesus (18:1–2). They might have been mentored by Paul, learning from him how to preach and teach the Scriptures, enabling them to explain to Apollos the way of God more accurately (18:29). Although they apparently raised up new believers in Ephesus, they did not mention anything about the Holy Spirit to these converts. The Ephesians

---

22. Unger, *Baptism*, 87.

The Related Themes and Their Applications

believed the gospel and became disciples without any prior knowledge of the Holy Spirit. These new believers were referred to as "disciples" (19:1), and Paul asked them, "Did you receive the Holy Spirit when you believed?" (19:2). From these comments and asking, it is obvious that these Ephesians were already believing disciples when Paul arrived.[23] Surprisingly, they answered that they had not even heard of the existence of the Holy Spirit. Paul asked again, "Into what were you baptized?" They said, "Into John's baptism." They were baptized into the name of John the Baptist. This means that they were the disciples of John. Paul explained to them that John's baptism was a baptism of repentance and told them to believe in Jesus as John, their teacher, taught them.

Jesus after his resurrection commanded his disciples to go to all the nations, baptizing them in the name of the Father and of the Son and of the Holy Spirit (Matt 28:19). Paul wrote in Romans 6 that believers are united with Christ in his death and resurrection by baptism. Believers are united with the body of Christ as members by baptism. Therefore, believers become his disciples by being baptized into the name of Jesus. Those Ephesian disciples needed to be united with Christ and to be the disciples of Christ, not of John, by being baptized in the name of the Father and of the Son and the Holy Spirit.

Paul laid his hands on them. At the same time, the Holy Spirit came on them and they began speaking in tongues and prophesying. We are not told how the Holy Spirit came down upon them. However, it is evident that they could have perceived and seen and heard the coming of the Holy Spirit. Thus, the Ephesian disciples might have experienced what John the Baptist, their teacher, prophesied and taught was being realized among themselves. The significant points here are Paul's laying his hands upon them and the Ephesians' both speaking in tongues and prophesying. From this the Ephesians could have confidence in Paul's saying and witness by their personal experience of speaking in tongues.

---

23. Lange, et al., *Acts*, 348–49.

His Touch on the Mouths

In Acts, however, this is an unusual case where the baptism is conducted by the apostles' laying on of hands.[24] The apostles prayed and laid their hands on the seven disciples who were chosen to be deacons at Jerusalem (Acts 6:6). They were specially chosen and appointed to serve the tables. When Ananias laid his hands on Saul, he regained his sight and was filled with the Holy Spirit. He immediately proclaimed Jesus in the synagogues (9:15–20). In view of these examples, the apostles and disciples laid their hands on the believers who were called for a special purpose in order to testify and witness to their call by God. The Ephesian disciples were prophesying when Paul laid his hands on them. Following this, the prophets prophesied by proclaiming, interpreting, and teaching the word of God in the synagogue and the hall of Tyrannus. Therefore, God had them prophesying to let them recognize their calling as his prophets in this case. Paul's laying his hands on the Ephesian disciples evidently brought the benefit of identifying himself to them as the servant of Christ. The twelve men who received the Holy Spirit and spoke in tongues at this time went on to participate in the evangelical meetings in the synagogue and later in the library of Tyrannous.

If this interpretation of the event is correct, God's purpose for sending the Holy Spirit and the gift of tongues and ability to prophesy was obviously not for their regeneration or sanctification, but instead, it was to confirm Paul's identity and the call of them to be prophets. It also served as proof of the truthfulness of their previous teachers, Apollos, Priscilla, and Aquila.

The Ephesian disciples were unaware of the existence of the Holy Spirit before Paul's visit. They became disciples by believing what they learned from their teachers. The word and the Spirit are inseparable, and the Holy Spirit comes and works in individuals when they may not even be conscious of it. Therefore, the Holy Spirit could have worked in the disciples when they first heard the word of God.[25] Thus, the gift of speaking in tongues that the Ephesians experienced served as a testimony of Paul's status as a

---

24. Pollhil, *Acts*, 400.
25. Calvin, *Institutes*, I.9.3.

The Related Themes and Their Applications

prophet from God and as a sealing of the disciples as prophets of the new covenant. The Ephesian disciples became believers by learning and believing the word of God, and by being baptized they were appointed to be the new covenant prophets by Paul's laying on of hands and by the witness and confirmation of the Holy Spirit sent by God.[26]

Three Thousand People Baptized at Pentecost

At the Pentecost event in Jerusalem, there were two specific occurrences. The first was the baptism of the Holy Spirit. The second was the baptism of three thousand souls by Peter and the disciples. When Peter, being baptized by the Holy Spirit and speaking in tongues, testified as a new covenant prophet, the people who heard him were cut to the heart and said, "Brothers, what shall we do?" (2:37). Peter replied that they should repent and be baptized in the name of Jesus for the forgiveness of sins, and then they would receive the gift of the Holy Spirit. They accepted his words and were baptized, and approximately three thousand souls were added to the church that day. However, it must be noted that there is no mention that these three thousand spoke in tongues when they were baptized. What explanation is there for this?

As was observed in the cases of Cornelius and the Ephesians, speaking in tongues was not a sign for the regeneration of the new believers. It was a sign for the apostles and disciples to be acknowledged as prophets sent by God. Peter and the other disciples were confirmed as spokesmen for God by the outpouring of the Holy Spirit upon them. As a result, people acknowledged their authority as God's prophets, and they accepted the disciples' words and followed them in baptism. There was no need for further signs to validate Peter's authority. The people did not need anything more to be saved but only to obey the word and be baptized.

It is clear from an examination and synthesis of the texts mentioned above that the baptism of the Holy Spirit at Pentecost

---

26. MacArthur, *Charismatic Chaos*, 186.

was an event that does not need to be repeated since it was an installation ceremony for the appointing and sealing of the disciples as new covenant prophets.

Traditional Reformed scholars have also maintained the non-repeatability of the event at Pentecost. They consider it to have been an event in redemptive history (*historia salutis*) that should not be squeezed into a grid for the application of redemption (*ordo salutis*).[27] These scholars regard the event at Pentecost as a fulfillment of the messianic coronation promised in Psalm 2:28. The coming of the Spirit is, therefore, evidence of the enthronement of Christ, just as the resurrection is evidence of the efficacy of the death of Christ as atonement for sin (Rom 4:24). The event at Pentecost is also the declaration of Christ as the Lord of Glory and an acknowledgement of Christ as the Mediator, evidenced by God sending the Spirit as Jesus asked. Pentecost, like the visible manifestation of coronation, is by its very nature *sui generis*. It is not any more repeatable as an event than is the crucifixion or the resurrection or the ascension of the Lord.[28] It is true that Jesus' death and resurrection and the coming of the Holy Spirit constitute the central theme of Christianity and account for one of the most important doctrines. However, importance alone is not enough to explain the non-repeatability of the baptism of the Holy Spirit. When Jesus was baptized by John the Baptist, he was enthroned as the Messiah and began his ministry as the King. His disciples confessed him as the Christ and as the Son of God during his lifetime (Matt 16:16; Mark 8:29; Luke 9:20). Before he was crucified, he asserted his kingship before Pilate, who hung a satirical notice above his head stating, "This is the King of the Jews" (Luke 23:38). His resurrection further proved this statement

---

27. Ferguson, *Holy Spirit*, 86–87.

28. Ferguson, *Holy Spirit*, 84–86. Reymond, as he explains the relationship between regeneration and the baptism of the Holy Spirit, attests to the non-repeatability of the event because he believes that the baptism of the Holy Spirit accompanying the speaking in tongues in Acts (Jews in ch.2, Samaritans in ch. 8, Cornelius—the Gentile—in ch.10, and the Ephesians in ch.19) serves to teach that all believers are all one body and one Spirit with Christ as in Eph 4:4–6. Reymond, *New Systematic Theology*, 64–65.

The Related Themes and Their Applications

(Acts 2:24, 32, 36). Before Pentecost, Jesus rose from the dead, appeared to his disciples, and gave them a prophetic mission, saying, "All authority in heaven and on earth has been given to me . . ." (Matt 28:18). The baptism of the Holy Spirit was then given to the disciples so that they might have authority and power to be new covenant prophets in order to be witnesses for Christ. Thus, the purpose of the baptism of the Holy Spirit at Pentecost was not as an application of redemption. Jesus accomplished our redemption on the cross. The event of Pentecost was for the installation of the disciples as his new covenant prophets. In that sense, it is not a repeatable occurrence. The traditional interpretation of Acts 2:3 has disregarded the Old Testament background regarding the appointment and installation of prophets, putting a disproportionate amount of theological emphasis on the event.

The Baptism of the Holy Spirit and Regeneration

Followers of the Reformed tradition, as they explain the experience of personal salvation, assert that the baptism of the Holy Spirit denotes an individual's acceptance of Christ as his Lord at the beginning of their conversion experience. Therefore, for them, the baptism of the Holy Spirit accords with regeneration. 1 Cor 12:13 is said to support this assertion.[29] In this regard, Ferguson states, "At the point of faith we participate individually in the effect of outpouring of the Spirit at Pentecost."[30] Packer asserts "that a great epochal transition in salvation-history took place at Pentecost and attempts to capture this transition in the following two statements: 'Jesus' disciples [e.g., Peter] were evidently Spirit-born believers [regenerated] prior to Pentecost, so their Spirit-baptism, which brought power to their life and ministry (Acts 1:8), was not the start of their spiritual experience.'"[31] Packer seems to be right in saying that Jesus' disciples were Spirit-born believers before

---

29. Ferguson, *Holy Spirit*, 84–86. Park, *Holy Spirit*, 106.
30. Ferguson, *Holy Spirit*, 85.
31. Packer, 145, quoted in Cole, *He Who Gives Life*, 195.

Pentecost, however, he seems to suggest the baptism in the Spirit is about power for life and service.

Even for Dunn, Pentecost is viewed as the inception of faith, and the spiritual state of the 120 assembled in the upper room prior to Pentecost was precisely that of Cornelius prior to his reception of the Spirit. Dunn further warns, "The life of the 120 prior to Pentecost cannot be used as a paradigm for the experience of today's new believer, precisely because that life was pre-Christian. Pentecost is itself a paradigm not of a second blessing, but of blessing for a Christian."[32]

However, all these assertions are made due to the error in translating Acts 2:3 and the subsequent interpretation of the baptism of the Holy Spirit. It should be interpreted as a ceremony of installation and sealing with the Spirit for the disciples as the new covenant prophets. Consequently, stating that believers were regenerated, or that a man comes to have faith by the baptism of the Holy Spirit at Pentecost, produces a great deal of confusion regarding an understanding of the role of the Holy Spirit. As Jesus taught, regeneration is being "born from above" (*gennēthē anōthen*, John 3:3), and being born above is the work of the Holy Spirit. Jesus explained to Nicodemus the mysteriousness and unpredictability of the Holy Spirit by comparing it to the wind (3:8). And he further explained that unless an individual is born of water and the Spirit, he cannot enter the kingdom of God (3:5). Then what is "the water and the Holy Spirit"? Larry Hart asserts that in "unless one is born of water and spirit" (*ean mē gennēthē ex hudatos kai pneumatos*), the preposition "*ex*" (ἐξ) takes both the water and the spirit as its objects, so it can be interpreted as "water of Spirit."[33] "In all probability, we have another hendiadys, one preposition governing the two nouns, water and spirit. Thus, a probable and helpful rendering would be "born of water and of the Spirit."[34] And he comments that this is another important reference then to Spirit baptism. Even though water is compared with the Holy Spirit as his inter-

---

32. Atkinson, *Baptism*, 11, 14–15. Dunn, *Baptism*, 51, 53.
33. Hart, "Spirit Baptism," 131.
34. Ibid.

The Related Themes and Their Applications

pretation, "water" in this instance, which contains the meaning of washing, refers to "the word of God," as referenced in the following passages (as well as Ezek 36:25–26; 47:1–12).

> He saved us not because of works done by us in righteousness, but according to his own mercy by the washing of regeneration and renewal of the Holy Spirit . . . (Titus 3:5)

> Already you are clean because of the word that I have spoken to you. (John 15:3)

> . . . that he might sanctify her, having cleansed her by the washing of water with the word . . . (Eph 5:26)

As the above verses show, there is an element of washing and renewal in regeneration. God cleanses us with the word and renews us with the Holy Spirit. Thus, the phrase "water and the Spirit" is analogous to "the word and the Spirit." Peter clearly taught that the word of God and the work of the Holy Spirit are the same in their role of regeneration of sinners: "since you have been born again [*anagennēmenoi*], not of perishable seed but imperishable, through the living and abiding word of God" (1 Pet 1:23).

Jesus' disciples are those who confessed Jesus as the Christ and the holy one of God while he was alive on earth (John 6:68; Matt 16:16; Mark 8:29; Luke 9:20). Jesus called them his family (Mark 3:34–35). They were those who were already bathed and clean (John 13:10). Since they were cleansed by the word of God, they were commanded to abide in him (John 15:3–4). Those who gathered together at one place at Pentecost were the family of Jesus. Paul stated that "no one can say 'Jesus is Lord' except in the Holy Spirit" (1 Cor 12:3) and "You, however, are not in the flesh but in the Spirit, if in fact the Spirit of God dwells in you. Anyone who does not have the Spirit of Christ does not belong to him" (Rom 8:9–10). These verses reveal that the disciples' confession of Jesus as the Christ was made possible by the work of the Holy Spirit, and that regeneration was completed by the work of the Holy Spirit prior to their confession. Jesus, upon hearing Peter's confession, said, "Blessed are you, Simon Bar-Jonah! For flesh and blood has not revealed this to you, but my Father who is in heaven" (Matt 16:17). Peter convinces us that the revelatory work of God was in them before his confession, and even before the event of Pentecost.[35] However, if we say that he is not regenerated yet and he was regenerated through the baptism of the Holy Spirit at Pentecost, then what is the ministry of Jesus in his lifetime?[36]

It is to be noted here that even though the word "regeneration" is not found in the Old Testament, the old covenant people had knowledge of what it was by the Holy Spirit. When Nicodemus could not understand what was meant by being "born again" by the Holy Spirit, Jesus said, "Are you the teacher of Israel and yet you do not understand these things?" (John 3:10). This reflects an acknowledgment that there was an awareness of the Holy Spirit's work among the people of Israel in restoring them to new life. As Cole points out, phrases such as "circumcised heart" (Deut 10:16; 30:6), "'heart of flesh' replacing 'hearts of stone'" (Ezek 36:26), and "a new spirit" (Jer 31:33)—all mentioned in the Old

---

35. A group of scholars, including Chafer, Carson, Gree, Pache, etc., suggest that the Spirit is certainly the key to Abraham's faith, but that it is going beyond the evidence to say that he was regenerated by the Spirit. For them, regeneration is a New Testament phenomenon. Even Pache maintains that there was no regenerative work of the Spirit in the lives of believers prior to Pentecost. Cole, *He Who Gives Life*, 144.

36. A group of scholars maintains based on John 7:37-39 that there was no activity of the Holy Spirit before the event of Pentecost because Jesus was not glorified yet. These verses have been brought the considerable debates among scholars. Jesus uses this figure to explain the coming of the Spirit to dwell in the believer. Traditionally the interpretation of these verses has been divided. The Eastern interpretation, following Origen, Athanasius, and other Greek fathers, and modern scholars such as Barrett, Behm, Bernard, Cadman, Carson, Lightfoot, Morris Schweizer, Turner, Westcott, and Zahn, understand that the believer himself becomes the source of the living water. However, the Western interpretation, which is also called the Christological interpretation and supported by Justin, Hippolytus, Tertullian, Irenaeus, Abbott, Beasley-Murray, Brown, Bultmann, Dodd, Dunn, Turner, Zerwick, etc., understands that Jesus himself is the source of the living water. The phrase "for as yet the Spirit had not been given, because Jesus was not yet glorified" does not mean that there was no activity of the Holy Spirit during the lifetime of Jesus, but that there were no dynamic activities of the Spirit as in Acts. Beasley-Murray, *John*, 115-17. NET, notes on John 7:38.

Testament—can be understood as having the same meaning as in the New Testament.[37] As for the interpretation of these phrases, certain theologians maintain that the Old Testament saints were not only regenerated by the Spirit, but that they were also indwelt by the Spirit.[38] Others hold that Old Testament saints were regenerated, but not indwelt, by the Spirit.[39] God is the God of creation, and he is also the God of renewing from the beginning.

God comes to individuals when they are not conscious of his presence, and he works in them to be born from above. The time and place of rebirth is not known. But by regeneration people are awakened to the fact that they are sinners, feeling their need for salvation and being made to believe in Jesus. This is not done by their participation in or as an effect of Pentecost. As has been stated above, this is not the purpose of Pentecost. Believers are regenerated before the baptism of the Holy Spirit.

The Baptism of the Holy Spirit and the Church

It is widely acknowledged among traditional theologians that the baptism of the Holy Spirit was an epoch-making event in the redemptive history of God. From the baptism of the Holy Spirit at Pentecost, the church came into being with a regenerated people, and a new age of a new covenant began. It is true that the disciples' work of proclaiming the word spread beyond the boundary of the Jews, the chosen people, to the Gentiles throughout the world, marking a new phase for the kingdom of God. However, the center of redemptive history is Christ. God promised the coming of the Christ and actually sent him at his appointed time. Therefore,

---

37. Beasley-Murray, *John*, 145.

38. Beasley-Murray, Goodwin, Owen, Warfield, and Gaffin, Ferguson, etc. Beasley-Murray states, ". . . what is patent in the New is latent in the Old. The need is one, the covenant of grace and the way of salvation is one, one faith that saves is one." According to this view, the Old Testament metaphor for "new birth" is the circumcision of the heart. *John*, 143–44.

39. Erickson, Van Gemeren, and Packer, etc., in Beasley-Murray, *John*, 144–45.

the coming of Christ should be regarded as the turning point in redemptive history. Here a more correct understanding of the text regarding the event of Pentecost is needed.

Dunn, along with other Protestant theologians, asserts that Pentecost inaugurated the age of the church, and the Spirit is the reality on which the church is founded.[40] On the basis of Acts 10:36; Rom 10:9; and 1 Cor 12:3 he sets forth a premise that the Christian church is a confessional church, and its basic confession is that Jesus is the Lord. But this confession only became possible after Jesus ascended to be the Lord and Christ (Acts 2:36) and received the Holy Spirit from the Father and then gave it to his disciples. He continues by saying that since the church was established for the evangelization of the world, the missionary invitation, "everyone who calls upon the name of the Lord shall be saved" (Acts 2:21), would be impossible. The four features of the primitive Christian community—apostolic teaching, *koinonia*, Christian water baptism in the name of Jesus Christ, and sharing a common meal, which may be included in the Lord's Supper—appeared after Pentecost. Therefore, for him the baptism of the Holy Spirit at Pentecost was the event when the disciples became true believers and the church inaugurated.[41] Thus, he proclaims, "The Church properly conceived did not come into existence until Pentecost."[42] According to Dunn, the 120 disciples who gathered in the upper room were not believers; neither was there a church at that time. If that is true, what was the spiritual status of the followers of Jesus before the event of Pentecost?

Jesus' disciples clearly confessed that he was the Christ, the Son of God, when they were asked about his identity by Jesus himself (Matt 16:16; Mark 8:29; Luke 9:20). In fact, Jesus blessed Peter after his confession and said, "Blessed are you, Simon Bar-Jona! For flesh and blood has not revealed this to you, but my Father who is in heaven" (Matt 16:17). He continued by telling Peter that

---

40. Schweizer, *TWNT*, 6:409. Stauffer, *New Testament Theology*, 165, quoted in Dunn, *Baptism*, 49.

41. Dunn, *Baptism*, 49–50.

42. Dunn, *Baptism*, 51.

The Related Themes and Their Applications

his church would be built on this rock. Jesus explicitly teaches that the revelation through the Holy Spirit had already been at work in the disciples. In his early ministry of the word, Jesus proclaimed to his biological brothers and sisters, who came to him after they had heard evil rumors about Jesus, that the disciples who heard the word of God and responded by doing the will of God would be his brothers and sisters and even his mother. Furthermore, he accepted such as his brothers and sisters (Mark 3:31–35). The Greek word *ekklēsia* (ἐκκλησία), translated as "church" in the New Testament, is translated from the Hebrew word *qāhāl*, which means "the assembly or congregation called by God." Stephen, a member of the Jerusalem church, said in his speech to the Jewish people, "This is the one who was in the congregation in the wilderness [*en tē ekklēsia en tē erēmō*] with the angel who spoke to him at Mount Sinai, and with our fathers" (Acts 7:38). Stephen, who was full of grace and power and spoke with wisdom and the Spirit (6:8, 10), said that the church existed from the time of their wilderness journey. The believers of the foundational church of Jerusalem said that the church came into being with the Sinai Covenant at the time of the exodus. The church comprises the people of Israel who made the covenant with God at Sinai after the exodus, and Jesus' disciples are connected to them through the continuity of their heritage. Furthermore, certain theologians trace the origin of the church back to the Trinitarian covenant before the creation and propose to acknowledge that the church originated in eternity past. Frame writes on the origin of the church as follows: "As a community of people worshiping God, the church goes back to the garden of Eden. After the fall, Cain and Abel brought sacrifice to the Lord, so then, too, there was the existence of a worshiping community. Seth, the third son of Adam and Eve, had as a son named Enosh. And Scripture tell us that 'at that time [the time of Seth and Enosh] people began to call upon the name of the Lord' (Gen 4:26)."[43]

However, some define the church as the eternal dwelling place of the Holy Spirit and identify the disciples gathered at the

---

43. Frame, *Systematic Theology*, 1017.

His Touch on the Mouths

upper room and baptized there by the Holy Spirit as the New Testament church and the beginning of the church. But Dunn, along with other Reformed scholars, asserts that the church had its inception at Pentecost. Even Bavinck calls Pentecost "the birthday of the Church" (*de geboortedag der gemeente*).[44] But in John 1:14 it says the word was made flesh and he tabernacled among us, and we saw his glory. If we do not separate the inseparable relationship of the Trinitarian God, the Son and the Holy Spirit, this event is viewed as an antitype of the Lord's coming to the tabernacle, which was built according to the command of God after Sinai covenant. Based on this relationship and continuity, Stephen called this covenant people the church. God the word became flesh, the Son, Jesus, to dwell among his people and pitched his tent on earth (John 1:14). Accordingly, Jesus' coming into his people and pitching his tent among them is related with the church of Mount Sinai. Jesus as the head of the new covenant came to this world to gather his people to him and establish his church with them (Matt 23:27).[45] He begins to gather his people by calling his disciples. Therefore, we cannot say that Pentecost is the beginning of the church.

Dunn, along with other Reformed theologians, maintains that the event of Pentecost is the beginning of the new covenant. However, this belief needs to be re-examined by looking at both the old covenant and the new covenant. The Lord delivered Israel from their bondage in Egypt and brought them to Mount Sinai. There he made a covenant with them by the sprinkling of blood. The people entered into a covenantal relationship whereby the Lord was the God of Israel and Israel was the people of the Lord. Thus, the people of Israel became the covenant people of the Lord, and the age of the covenant was instituted. The Old Testament portrays the covenantal relationship with various metaphors, such as husband and wife, father and son, a king and his people, a shepherd and sheep, and a divine warrior and his levied army.[46] However,

---

44. Bavinck, *Magnalia Dei*, 442.

45. The theme of God's gathering his people is also found in Deut 30:3; Ps 147:2; Isa 11:12; 27:13; 56:8; Ezek 39:18.

46. Cf. Sohn, *Divine Election*, 10 and *YHWH*, 1.

The Related Themes and Their Applications

Israel did not remain faithful to the covenant, and God poured out a covenant curse on Israel, promising to give them a new one (Jer 31:31–34). He declared, "I will put my law within them, and I will write it on their hearts. And I will be their God, and they shall be my people" (31:33). He promised that he would renew his unchangeable and unbreakable relationship with his people. Afterward, at the appointed time, God the word came to his people as Jesus and sowed the seed of the word in the hearts of his people, making a new covenant with his disciples at the Passover table. At the meal, Jesus took the bread and broke it and gave it to his disciples, saying, "This is my body, which is given for you. Do this in remembrance of me." And after they had eaten, Jesus said, "This cup that is poured out for you is the new covenant in my blood" (Luke 22:19–20; cf. Matt 26:28; Mark 15:24). He made this new covenant with his disciples by breaking his body and shedding his blood, just as the animal's body was cut and its blood sprinkled at the time the old covenant was made at Mount Sinai. Following these statements, Jesus gave his disciples the new commandment that they were to love each other (John 13:34). Just as the theme of the Ten Commandments of the old covenant was to love God and their neighbors, Jesus also gave the commandment of love to his disciples after he made the new covenant. The love relationship between God and his people, and among the people themselves, is the main theme of both covenants. If the old covenant emphasized legal and formal relationships, as in the case of marriage in Jer 31:31–34, the new covenant emphasized a personal and internal love relationship beyond the boundary of legal force. Therefore, Jesus commanded, "Abide in me, and I in you" (John 15:4) so that "they may all be one, just as you, Father, are in me, and I in you, that they also may be in us, so that the world may believe that you have sent me" (17:21). He wanted us to have a relationship characterized by an inseparable, organic, and mutual indwelling love with the Father and the Son. Jesus created and concluded the covenant by shedding his blood on the cross. Therefore, the death of Jesus on the cross was the rite that initiated the covenant, and the new covenant came into force from the moment of his death.

The tearing of the temple curtain in two (Luke 23:45) signified the initiation of the validity of the new covenant. It signified the end of ceremonial and ritual law of the old covenant.[47] Thus, the new covenant began from the moment of Jesus' death on the cross, not at the time of the baptism of the Holy Spirit at Pentecost. In Jesus' day, Pentecost was a Jewish celebration memorializing the day that the Jewish people had received the law at Mount Sinai, fifty days after the exodus. According to Dunn, when the Holy Spirit came at Pentecost, God fulfilled the promise of a new covenant, which had been foretold by Jeremiah when he wrote that God would write his law on the hearts of his people.[48] Therefore, he asserts that Pentecost is the starting point for the new covenant. However, scholars have not yet arrived at a consensus regarding the relationship between the event at Mount Sinai and the Jewish feast of Pentecost at the time of Jesus.

The Baptism of the Holy Spirit and the Baptism of Water

People in the Reformed tradition commonly acknowledge that the baptism of the Holy Spirit refers to an individual's acceptance of Jesus Christ as his/her savior. 1 Cor 12:13 supports this view, which claims that at the moment of the baptism of the Holy Spirit a sinner is regenerated and united with Christ, becoming a member of his body. They further explain that "at the moment of faith, we participate individually in the effect of the outpouring of the Spirit at Pentecost."[49] MacArthur uses the same line of reasoning and says, "When the Holy Spirit came at Pentecost a new order was established. From then on, the Holy Spirit came to every believer at the moment of faith and indwelt the believer in permanent, abiding relationship."[50] People who accept this explanation interpret 1

---

47. Stein, *Luke*, 595–96.
48. Dunn, *Baptism*, 47. Atkinson, *Baptism*, 10–11, 52–54.
49. Ferguson, *Holy Spirit*, 85.
50. MacArthur, *Charismatic Chaos*, 178.

The Related Themes and Their Applications

Cor 12:13 as applying to the event of Pentecost. This puts excessive weight on the once-for-all character of the baptism of the Holy Spirit, identifying it with Christ's birth, death, and resurrection. Furthermore, they contend that the baptism of the Holy Spirit is an epoch-making event in redemptive history.

However, their interpretation of 1 Cor 12:13 needs further examination: "For in one Spirit we were all baptized into one body [*kai gar en heni pneumatic hēmeis pantes eis hen sōma ebaptisthēmen*]—Jews or Greeks, slaves or free—and all were made to drink of one spirit." As has been explained above, the Holy Spirit had already worked in the lives of Jesus' disciples, and they had experienced regeneration prior to being baptized by the Holy Spirit. They were able to come to the upper room by faith because of this regeneration. Therefore, the above verse should not be interpreted as if everyone together became one body belonging to Christ at a single moment in history as the result of the baptism of the Holy Spirit. The phrase "in one Spirit we were all baptized into one body" means that believers became one church, the body of Christ, not by a different Spirit, but by the same Spirit.[51]

As discussed above, regeneration is not concomitant with the baptism of the Spirit at Pentecost. If this is an accurate interpretation, then when do believers who are living after the event of Pentecost receive the baptism of the Holy Spirit? The answer is at the time of baptism by water. Baptism by water is a visible symbol of the baptism of the Holy Spirit. At the time of Jesus' baptism by John the Baptist, Jesus saw the Holy Spirit descended on him in bodily form like a dove, and he heard a voice from heaven say, "You are my beloved Son, with you I am well pleased" (Luke 3:22). This event is widely acknowledged as the inauguration ceremony of Jesus as the Messiah. Shortly thereafter, Jesus proclaimed the beginning of his ministry by quoting from Isaiah during the Sabbath service in the synagogue at Nazareth:

> The Spirit of the Lord is upon me, because he has anointed me, to proclaim good news to the poor. He has sent

---

51. Calvin, *Corinthians*, 1:406. Thiselton, *Corinthians*, 998–1001. Garland, *1 Corinthians*, 591. Knowling, "Acts," 890–891. Johnson, *1 Corinthians*, 231.

> me to proclaim liberty to the captives and recovering
> of sight to the blind, to set at liberty those who are op-
> pressed, to proclaim the year of the Lord's favor. (Luke
> 4:18–19; cf. Isa 61:1–2; 58:6)

When he finished reading from the scroll, Jesus proclaimed, "Today this Scripture has been fulfilled in your hearing" (Luke 4:21). These verses from the book of Isaiah were about Jesus himself, the Messiah, just as he said. Accordingly, his baptism by water was a symbol of the anointing of him to proclaim the good news, and the sealing of the Holy Spirit witnessed this appointment for him to be the one sent by God to save his people.

In the same way, a believer is baptized by the Holy Spirit at the time of his/her baptism by water. The believer receives his new office as a prophet of the new covenant at this time, and the authority to carry out this mission is testified at the ceremony of baptism by water. Thus, the command of Jesus to make disciples by going, baptizing, and teaching what they have learned was given in order to make them prophets of the new covenant. Since baptism by water and the baptism of the Holy Spirit occur simultaneously, new disciples are appointed and testified by baptism. At this time, believers are united with Christ in his death and resurrection (Rom 6:1–11), becoming members of his body, the church. In baptism, believers proclaim publically that they have become Christian, and thus they have a new status and identity.[52]

Jesus called Saul, who had been persecuting his disciples, while he was on the road to Damascus by means of a strong light that focused on Saul and blinded him. Jesus then appointed Saul to be his chosen instrument to proclaim his name before the Gentiles, kings, and children of Israel by the laying on of hands by Ananias. Saul was then baptized with both water and the Holy Spirit and was installed as a new covenant prophet and servant of the word. The word "immediately" in Acts 9:18 signifies the simultaneousness of both baptisms. However, the phrase "to be filled with the Holy Spirit" does not refer to Jesus' appointment of Saul as a prophet. Rather, it refers to the gift of the Holy Spirit that was

---

52. Brownson, *Promise of Baptism*, 52.

The Related Themes and Their Applications

essential for Saul to be able to accomplish his Gentile ministry. For Saul, regeneration, baptism by water, and baptism by the Holy Spirit were all given concurrently.[53]

In light of the above discussions, it is clear that baptism by water is a visible sign of regeneration, our new life in Christ. Believers publically enter into union with Christ in his death and resurrection at the time of baptism by water. New life with Christ is not a future event to be realized. It is a reality that has already happened, just as Paul confessed in Galatians 2:20, "I have been crucified with Christ. It is no longer I who live, but Christ who lives in me." Therefore, a believer should consider himself to be regenerated at the time he is baptized by water, and simultaneously he is baptized by the Holy Spirit in order to receive the office of a new covenant prophet with the accompanying authority necessary to accomplish the mission he has been given.[54] Jesus began his ministry as the prophet when he was baptized by water and the Holy Spirit, and he finished it by commanding his disciples after giving them the baptism of the Holy Spirit to baptize the new converts to be new covenant prophets.

The Baptism of the Holy Spirit and the Fullness of the Holy Spirit

One of the key contentions of the Pentecostal is the impossibility of making a distinction between the baptism of the Holy Spirit and the fullness of the Holy Spirit. They understood Spirit baptism "as the coming of God's Spirit into the believer's life in a very focused way. Down through church history there were occasional incidents

---

53. There are many discussions among scholars regarding the theme of Acts 9. Is it a description of Paul's conversion, his call, or both? The common point for those who allege it is primarily about the similarity of Paul's call in this chapter with the call narrative of Old Testament prophets in Isa 6:1–13; Jer 1:4–10, etc. However, Paul's experience is a typical example of the Gentiles' call to be prophets of God subsequent to their regeneration, followed by baptism by water. Barrett, *Acts*, 1:439–45.

54. WCF, ch. 28. Shorter Catechism, q. 94, and Larger Catechism, q. 165, in WCF.

of Pentecostal experiences."[55] And they said that both 120 disciples and three thousand converts were filled with the Holy Spirit and had "a full, satisfying experience" at Pentecost. According to them, Bible uses a variety of terms with these phrases, such as "pouring out of the Spirit in Joel (Acts 2:17–21), a receiving (and active taking) of a gift (Acts 2:38), a falling upon (Acts 8:16; 10:14; 11:15), pouring out of the gift (Acts 10:45), and a coming upon." With this variety of terms, they assert that it is impossible to suppose there is any difference between the baptism and the filling.[56]

Jesus' disciples were given the authority to teach and proclaim the word of God by being baptized with the Holy Spirit at Pentecost. People could recognize them as men of God when they spoke the word because it was accompanied by the experience of speaking in tongues. At the moment when they were preaching, the Bible states, the disciples were filled with the Holy Spirit. This reminds us that where the word was preached, the Holy Spirit descended powerfully and worked strongly among them. After healing the lame at the Beautiful Gate and preaching to the crowds at the temple, Peter and John were arrested, imprisoned, and examined the next day by the council. At the hearing, Peter was asked by what power or by what name he had healed the crippled man. At the time of his reply, Peter was said to be filled with the Holy Spirit (Acts 4:8). Jesus had promised that he would give the baptism of the Holy Spirit and send a Helper for occasions such as this. After Peter and John were released, they went to their friends, reported the event, and prayed. "When they had prayed, the place in which they were gathered together was shaken, and they were all filled with the Holy Spirit and continued to speak the word of God with boldness" (4:31). In a later incident, Stephen, a member of the Jerusalem church, was so full of grace and power that no one could withstand the wisdom and Spirit with which he was speaking (6:8, 10).

It should be noted here that the believers in Jerusalem prayed for the disciples to speak the word of God with boldness, and they

---

55. Horton, "Spirit Baptism," 47.
56. Horton, "Spirit Baptism," 59.

The Related Themes and Their Applications

were filled with the Holy Spirit when they preached the word of God. Thus, there is an obvious relationship between the witness of the word and the fullness of the Holy Spirit. The Holy Spirit works when the word is preached. The disciples had already been baptized with the Holy Spirit, but they were filled with the Holy Spirit when they preached. In most cases, the people who heard the preaching of the disciples were not filled with the Holy Spirit, but only those who preached were filled with it (2:4; 4:9; 6:10, 55; 10:44–45; 11:12, etc.). This pattern can be seen throughout the book of Acts in the evangelical ministry of the apostles and disciples.

Therefore, the fullness of the Holy Spirit comes to those disciples who are working for the ministry of the word. Man cannot control the Holy Spirit. However, where the word is preached, the Holy Spirit actively works there, because the word and the Spirit are inseparable. The Spirit of God cannot be commanded to come and work at the bidding of the believer. The Holy Spirit goes where the word goes and begins to work where the word remains. Thus, given this nature of the Spirit and the word, if one wants to be filled with the Holy Spirit, then it is necessary to be filled with the word of God. In this paradigm one can discern the reason for the powerful activities of the Holy Spirit in the Jerusalem church. Acts 2:42 states that they "devoted themselves to the apostles' teaching and the fellowship, to the breaking of bread and the prayers." In 6:4, as the apostles appoint the seven deacons they say, "It is not right that we should give up preaching the word of God to serve tables." They continue, saying, "We will devote ourselves to prayer and to the ministry of the word" (6:4). The result of this focus on the word of God was that "the word of God continued to increase, and the number of the disciples multiplied greatly in Jerusalem, and a great many of the priests became obedient to the faith" (6:7). Luke makes it clear that the amazing growth of the Jerusalem church was a direct result of the apostles' focus on the word. Because the word was boldly preached, the Holy Spirit worked powerfully among them. The two working together brought about the notable growth of the church. Accordingly, Luke seems to say throughout the entire book that the acts of the apostles were mainly acts of the word, rather than of the Holy Spirit (1:8; 2:42; 6:7; 12:24; 13:1–3; 17:11; 19:20; 28:23; 30:31). Strictly speaking, the book of Acts details the "Acts of the word," rather than the "Acts of the Holy Spirit."

These thoughts notwithstanding, it should be noted that the fullness of the Holy Spirit is mentioned in the context of personal sanctification and service to the church. Paul exhorts the Ephesians to be filled with the Holy Spirit (Eph 5:18). Since this exhortation is in a passive form, the command is something that cannot be achieved by personal will and effort. It is clear that the fullness of the Spirit has nothing to do with the event of personal regeneration as the baptism of the Holy Spirit. Nevertheless, it is a requirement for all believers to live and enjoy a dynamic Christian life. How, then, can one be filled with the Holy Spirit and bear abundant spiritual fruit? Traditionally, the pastors have taught the inseparability of the word and the Spirit.[57] The apostle Paul commanded, "Let the word of Christ dwell in you richly" (*Ho logos tou Christou enoikeitō en hymin plousiōs*, Col 3:16). The Greek word *enoikeō* (ἐνοικέω) means "to dwell in" and is used to refer to the indwelling of the Holy Spirit as in 2 Tim 1:14, "By the Holy Spirit who dwells with us [*pneumatos hagiou tou enoikountos en hemin*], guard the good deposit entrusted to you." Thus, the fullness of the Holy Spirit is used in conjunction with the indwelling of the word. The Westminster Standards emphasize the unity of the word of God and the Spirit of God. The summary statement of the Confessions is that God's word and God's Spirit "only do sufficiently and effectively reveal [God] unto man of their salvation" (WLC, q. 2).[58] Thus, if anyone wants to be filled with the Holy Spirit, it can be accomplished by letting the word dwell within himself. Reymond further describes the relationship between the word and the Spirit:

---

57. Calvin, *Institutes*, 19.3. Ferguson, "John Owen," 105–6. Goold, ed. *Works of John Owen*, 3, 192.

58. This unity is referred to seven times in the Confession (1.5, 6, 10; 8.8; 10.1; 14.1; 27.3), seven times in the Larger Catechism (q. 2, 4, 43, 67, 72,76, 155), and once in the Shorter Catechism (q. 24). Morecraft, "Holy Spirit," 249–50.

The Related Themes and Their Applications

These two ideas, both highlighting a divine, subjective influence, are practically identical. To be filled with the Spirit is to be indwelt by the word of Christ; to be indwelt by the word of Christ is to be filled with the Spirit. One must never separate the Spirit from Christ's word, or Christ's word from the Spirit. The Spirit works by and with Christ's word. Christ's word works by and with the Spirit.[59]

Therefore, believers are to seek to be filled with the Holy Spirit by letting the word of God dwell in them throughout their lifetime, just as the Lord commanded Ezekiel (Ezek 3:2). The fullness of the Holy Spirit is the gift of God to the believer for his personal sanctification and for the service of his church. This is attained by letting the word of God richly dwell within him.

The Gifts of the Holy Spirit

Peter answered to people asking what they should do after listening his speech, "Repent and be baptized every one of you in the name of Jesus Christ, for the forgiveness of your sins, and you will receive the gift of the Holy Spirit" (Acts 2:38). Peter said here they would receive the gift of the Holy Spirit (*tēn dōrean tou hagiou pneumatos*), not just the Holy Spirit. Jesus told them they would receive the Holy Spirit (Acts 1:5), but Peter said "they will receive the gift of the Holy Spirit." On that day the three thousand people who received the word of Peter were baptized but there was no mention of their speaking in tongues. Accordingly, it is evident that the word "Holy Spirit" is used in distinction from the baptism of the Holy Spirit and the gift of the Holy Spirit. As we observed before, the baptism of the Holy Spirit is used for Jesus' baptism by John the Baptist as well as the installation of Jesus' disciples as the new covenant prophets. Its usage is very limited. Then what is the gift of the Holy Spirit? It is a free gift or benefit including eternal life and the Holy Spirit given by God for the believers. The gift of the Holy Spirit (*hē dōrea tou hagiou pneumatos*) that Peter

---

59. Reymond, *New Systematic Theology*, 766.

mentioned in Acts 2:38 is referring to the individual salvation (cf. Rom 3:24; 5:17; Eph 3:7; 2 Cor 11:7 etc.). However, in 1 Cor 12:9, 28, 30, 31 the Greek text uses only *charisma* for "the gifts," and the "the Holy Spirit" (*tou hagiou pneumatos*) is not used with it. In English versions, *dōrea* and *charisma* are translated "gift," and it brings some confusion to the reader. In the New Testament the word *dōrea* is used only for the spiritual or supernatural gift freely given by God to man, such as for eternal life (John 4:10), the Holy Spirit (Acts 2:38), righteous relationship with God (Rom 5:17), etc.[60] The Greek noun *charisma* is a derivative of *charizomai* ("to give") and means "what has been given." It is usually used as what has been given by the result of God's gracious act (Rom 11:29; 2 Cor 1:11; Rom 5:15-16). In some cases it is referring to a special ability that was given when a believer was appointed and installed to a certain office (2 Tim 4:14; 1Pet 4:10).[61] Even though it is not easy to make sharp distinction between the two words and their usages, δωρεά is used for the salvation of the natural man (Rom 3:24; Eph 3:7; 2Cor 11:7) and *charisma* for the believers to serve the church. The gift (*charisma*) that Paul mentions in 1 Cor 12 is used for the special abilities or talents given to the members of body, the church, in order to play the function assigned by God. Accordingly, the baptism of the Holy Spirit, which was to seal the appointee as a new covenant prophet, is to be distinguished from the gifts (of the Holy Spirit), which was given to the believers in order for them to perform their role as a member of the church.

Paul is comparing the relationship between the church and the believers with the body of Christ and members as he teaches the gifts in 1 Cor 12:4-6:

> Now there are varieties of gifts, but the same Spirit; and there are varieties of service, but the same the Lord; there

---

60. The lexical meaning of δωρεά is "gift," "free gift," "benefit"; in the NT it is used only of spiritual and supernatural gifts that are freely given by God to believers, including eternal life (John 4:10), the Holy Spirit (Acts 2:38), righteousness, i.e., the state of being put right with God (Rom 5:17), enabling grace for appointed ministry (Eph 3:7). Friberg et al., *Analytical Lexicon*, 122.

61. Ibid. 407.

The Related Themes and Their Applications

are varieties of activities, but it is the same God who empowers them all in everyone.

Though gifts, services, and activities are different, these are all from the God of Trinity, same Spirit, same Lord, and same God. In 1 Cor 12:7 Paul says that God's purpose for the gifts is "for the common good." Paul here emphasizes that the purpose of the Trinitarian God giving the gift to each person (*ekastō*) is not for the individual's benefit, but "for the profit of all" (*pros to symperon*).

In verses 8–10 Paul listed the varieties of the gifts: the utterance of wisdom, the message of knowledge, faith, healing by the one Spirit, the working of the miracles, prophecy, the ability to distinguish between the spirits, various kinds of tongues, and the interpretation of tongues. Here he again repeated that they were given "by the same Spirit" (*kata auto pneuma*). It is to be noted here that the phrase "by the same Spirit" (*en tō auto pneumati*) and "by the one Spirit" (*en tō heni pneumati*) are repeated with same meaning and verse 11 repeatedly summarizes as, "All these are empowered by one and the same Spirit, who apportions to each one individually as he wills."

From verse 12 Paul compares the relationship between the church and believers to the body of Christ and its members and says that "in one Spirit we were all baptized into one body." Here "one Spirit" means "the same Spirit" as mentioned above and "to be baptized" describes a ritual ceremony symbolizing union with Christ. Therefore, the meaning of the word "baptism" here is different in meaning from the baptism of the Holy Spirit. The Holy Spirit plays the role of binding the believers to the body of Christ and the water baptism is the visible ceremony symbolizing the union. As we have various members in our body, the same is the case with the church. From this analogy Paul declares, "Now you are the body of Christ and individually members of it" (v. 27). Then, what kinds of members are there in the body?

Before he goes on to explain the kinds of members, Paul explains the relationship between the body and its members and their functions and characters. First of all, there is one body with many members (12:12-23). God arranged the members in the body, each one of them as he chose (v. 18), and distributed a unique role to each member. Second, therefore, there is no distinction of importance between members in the body. The one member cannot say to the other, "I have no need of you." God has composed the body that there may be no division and may have the same care for one another (v. 25). Third, the body and members share the same suffering and honor together, even between the members (v. 26). They therefore are organically related and inseparable. Following these principles, Paul declares, "Now you are the body of Christ and individually members of it." And he listed the members that God appointed in the Church, "first apostles, second prophets, third teachers, then miracles, then gifts of healing, helping, administrating, and various kind of tongues" (v. 28). What is to be noted here is that for apostles, prophets, and teachers, Paul made a list of referring to man and his office, whereas miracles, healing, helping, administering, and tongues are categorized as God-given gifts to anyone according to his good will. Paul is not seen here to show any graded hierarchical list in the gifts.

What is to be noted here is that the word "tongue" refers to "various kind of tongues" (*gene glōssōn*, v. 28). This suggests the existence of various tongues. Paul's point here seems to be that all believers cannot have the same office and that all people cannot have the same gifts. Thus, he raised rhetorical questions that lead to the same answer, "no": "Are all apostles? Are all prophets? Are all teachers? Do all work miracles? Do all possess gifts of healing? Do all speak with tongues? Do all interpret?" (vv. 29-30). However, Paul seems to suggest that there exists the consciousness of a hierarchical difference among the offices and gifts in the church, even though he teaches that there are "no distinctions" in the gifts of God to his saints. Thus, he teaches his Corinthian brothers to desire earnestly the higher gifts, and he says that he will show them a still more excellent way. According to Paul, faith, hope, and love are the higher gifts, and among these the greatest is love (13:1-13). He exhorts them to pursue love (14:1). The members created by God should be unified and maintained by love and bear fruit. The

The Related Themes and Their Applications

body of Christ is a living being with a heart beating with love. Among the gifts of God, tongues and prophecies have been the objects of debate throughout the world in history. We need further discussions on these subjects.

Tongues

The teachings on tongues are found in Mark 16:7; Acts 2;10;19; and 1 Cor 12–14.[62] Paul particularly deals with tongues and guides us to understand the principle and practices.

Tongues as the Gifts

Paul teaches about the gifts in 1 Cor 12 and mentions tongues lastly in the list. The tongues spoken at Pentecost were evidence of the baptism of the Holy Spirit ordaining Jesus' disciples to seal them as the new covenant prophets at the appointed place, and the tongues spoken there were foreign languages. Jesus and his disciples spoke the Galilean dialect, but the people who came from all over the world were hearing the disciples speak each in their own language (Acts 2:6). Thus, they were bewildered, amazed, and astonished (vv. 7–12). We don't know exactly what language the family of Cornelius and the disciples of Ephesus spoke, but the tongues spoken by the Corinthians seem to be different in their nature and character from those of the disciples in Jerusalem at Pentecost. At Jerusalem, the people could understand directly in their own language what the disciples were speaking without interpreters. The

---

62. For charismatics, Romans 8:26–27 is also one of the New Testament passages referring to the Holy Spirit: "Likewise the Spirit helps us in our weakness. For we do not know what to pray for as we ought, but the Spirit himself intercedes for us with groanings too deep for words. And he who searches hearts knows what is the mind of the Spirit, because the Spirit intercedes for the saints according to the will of God." According to many scholars, "with groanings too deep for words" refers to an ordinary normal language, and not to speaking in tongues or praying in tongues. The Holy Spirit prays for us. He does not translate our prayer in tongues and deliver it to God. MacArthur, *Charismatic Chaos*, 224 n. 11.

Corinthian tongues, however, needed an interpreter. Furthermore, speaking in tongues did not build up the church at Corinth, but instead brought about conflicts among the believers.[63]

Then what is a tongue? In 1 Cor 14:2 Paul explains that a man speaking in a tongue speaks not to men but to God, and no one understands him as he utters mysteries in the Spirit. Therefore, a tongue is individual spiritual communication with God. A man speaking in tongues can pray in tongues (v. 14) and give thanks with his spirit (v. 16). However, if a man prays in a tongue, his spirit prays but his mind will be unfruitful (v. 14). Paul further says, "If with your tongue your speech is not intelligible, how will anyone know what is said? For you will be speaking into the air" (v. 9), and if anyone does not know the meaning of the language, he will be a foreigner (barbarian) to the speaker and the speaker a foreigner (a barbarian) to him (v. 11). The Corinthian believers were speaking with a tongue that was unintelligible. Even so, we cannot say that the tongue was a heavenly language. God spoke a normal human language when he spoke to his people, such as Abraham, Moses, and others. Jesus also spoke in a normal language, and while he prayed to God at Gethsemane (John 17) he spoke in a plain human language that his disciples could hear and understand. But the Corinthians spoke neither normal tongues nor heavenly tongues. Because of this, some scholars called the Corinthian tongues counterfeit tongues since they modified the Pentecostal tongues. Because counterfeit tongues were used in ecstasy or in the state of unconsciousness, they are said to be a modification or a deterioration of the Pentecostal tongues.[64] Taking this into consideration, it

63. According to Robertson, since the Greek word γλῶσσα means "tongue" and is used for both the event of Pentecost at Jerusalem and for the Corinthian phenomenon, both tongues spoken at Jerusalem and Corinth are the same. Notably, the Corinthian tongues were essentially the same because they were interpretable by a contemporary language. From this viewpoint, the tongues of modern believers are different from those of the New Testament. *Final Word*, 33–37. According to Bruner's observation, "speaking in tongues in Acts is on all three occasions a corporate, church-founding, group-conversion phenomenon and never the subsequent Spirit-experience of individual." Bruner, *Theology*, 192, quoted in Unger, *Baptism*, 88.

64. Samarin, *Tongues*, xii, 227. Cf. MacArthur, *Charismatic Chaos*, 228.

is true that there is some similarity between the tongues of Corinth and those of Pentecost, but there are also differences. The modern charismatic tongues are more like those of the Corinthian church. However, we cannot deny the practice of speaking in tongues in the churches today regard them as unorthodox or pagan.[65] Paul says, "I thank God that I speak in tongues more than all of you. Nevertheless, in church I would rather speak five words with my mind in order to instruct others, than ten thousand words in a tongue" (1 Cor 14:18-19).[66] And he teaches the guideline for speaking in tongues in the church.

The Rules for Speaking in Tongues

The church is the body of Christ and the believers are the members of the body. In order for the body to be healthy, each of the members of the body should accomplish its role faithfully. God gave to each one of the members different gifts of the Holy Spirit. Speaking in tongues is one of the gifts. But he gave rules for using these gifts.

---

65. Some scholars attest that at the end of the apostolic age speaking in tongues ceased because of completion of the canon. Warfield, *Counterfeit Miracles*, and Chantry, *Signs of Apostles*, cited in Robeck, *ISBE*, 4:872. However, there are also those who are against cessation of the tongues. Carson argues that "the tongues spoken at Pentecost and those spoken in Corinth were not essentially different. That is to say, they were real languages with cognitive content but serving different function. For example, the tongues of Pentecost could be understood by bystanders. However, the tongues at Corinth needed interpretation and consisted of a special form of coded utterance." *Showing the Spirit*, 83–86. Along with Carson, see Deere, *Surprised by the Power of the Spirit*; Fee, *God's Empowering Presence*, 204–8; Fee, *1 Corinthians*, 642–46.

66. However, Horton insists that the Pentecostal revival and its charismatic counterpart have continued to spread, as he quotes from George's assertion: "To argue that Charismatic gifts were necessary only for the first century Church and that they were not needed today in our individual and corporate worship is contrary to the teachings of the Scriptures as well as the experience of millions of Pentecostal/ Charismatic believers who are living in all continents of the world." George, *Dimensions of Spirituality*, 27, quoted in Horton, "Spirit Baptism," 83.

First, it is to be noted that there is no command prohibiting speaking in tongues. As he compares tongues with prophecy, Paul asks, "What then, brothers?" and says, "When you come together each one has a hymn, a lesson, a revelation, a tongue, or an interpretation. Let all things be done for building up" (1 Cor 14:26). This verse presupposes the existence of tongues and revelations in the church.[67] After his resurrection, Jesus told his disciples, "Go into all the world and proclaim the gospel to the whole creation" (Mark 16:15), and he continued to say, "And these signs will accompany those who believe: in my name they will cast out demons; they will speak in new tongues . . ."(v. 17). This promise of Jesus does not seem to be referring to the time of Pentecost. In particular, Jesus seems to mention "speaking in new tongues" in reference to the signs and wonders shown among the believers who heard the gospel proclaimed by the disciples and believed.

Paul gives thanks to God saying, "I thank God that I speak in tongues more than anyone else" (v. 18). He states, "Now I want you all to speak in tongues" (v. 5). In verse 39 he exhorts, "So my brothers, earnestly desire to prophesy, and do not forbid speaking in tongues." Thus, Paul did not prohibit speaking in tongues and positively expressed his hope for all the Corinthian believers to speak in tongues. However, it seems clear that the Corinthians' speaking in tongues brought about many problems in the church. Therefore, Paul teaches them to desire earnestly to prophesy more than to speak in tongues.

Second, speaking in tongues should build up the church. Paul repeatedly emphasized, "Strive to excel in building up the church" (v. 12); "Let all things be done for building up" (v. 26); and ". . .

---

67. Thiselton discusses "revelation" as follows: "ἀποκάλυψις, 1 Cor. 14:26, NRSV, REB, NIV, NJB, KJV/AV) seems to suggest an act of divine disclosure on the spot. The word may indeed include this, but it does not exclude the communication of what came to be revealed by God through some experience or through biblical reflection prior to the act of worship itself." *The First Epistle to the Corinthians*. Gerland gives his opinion about revelation and tongue: "Revelation" refers to something divinely disclosed and presented in comprehensible language. The revelation could occur prior to or during the worship (cf. 2 Cor. 12:17; Gal. 1:12, 16; 2:2). The 'tongue' is spontaneous as is the 'interpretation' of what it means." *1 Corinthians*.

The Related Themes and Their Applications

all things should be done decently and in order" (v. 40). Believers should speak in tongues for the purpose of building up the church. All members should build up the body of the church, and their actions should profit the church. But if one member emphasizes his role too much and does not take into account the other members, the body will be abnormal, and the result will be conflict and destruction. Paul acknowledges speaking in tongues in the church as being a gift of God. However, he is in doubt as to whether or not it will build up the church. He proclaims, "the one who speaks in a tongue will build up himself, but the one prophesies builds up the church" (v. 4). Here the Greek word *oikodomeō* means "to build," "to restore," and "to edify." Putting these together, the meaning of "to build up" is essentially to help in the growth and development of the church. Accordingly, we can say that speaking in tongues will build up an individual, but not all in the church. Therefore, those who are eager for manifestations of the Spirit are strongly advised to strive to excel in building up the church (v. 12).

Third, Paul teaches the necessity of an interpreter. "If any speak in a tongue, let there be only two or at most three, and each in turn, and let someone interpret" (v. 27). Speaking in tongues is not the collective outpouring of indistinguishable and unintelligible speech. Only two or three persons can speak in tongues by turns in the church. Thus, one person speaks in tongues and the other should interpret it. If there is no interpreter, each one of them should keep silent in the church and speak to himself and to God (v. 28). Without an interpreter, speaking in tongues will not give any benefit to the speaker, and it will be like speaking in the air (v. 6). Therefore, if both the speaker and the listener cannot understand what is being said, they will be like barbarians to each other (v. 11). The church should build up the character and cultivate the personality of believers, instead of bringing them down to the level of barbarians. The Greek word *barbaros* means "to speak a foreign language" or "speak an unintelligent language." It refers to that incommunicable state when foreigners first meet together. Accordingly, if there is no interpreter, all the believers should be quiet in the church (v. 28). The women speaking in tongues are more in number than the men in the Corinthian church. That is why Paul seems to command the women to be quiet in the church.

Fourth, tongues are signs not for the believers but for unbelievers. Paul writes, "If, therefore, the whole church come together, and all speak in tongues, and outsiders or unbelievers enter, will they not say that you are out of your minds?" (v. 23). And as at Pentecost, they will mock the believers as being drunkards filled with sweet wine (Acts 2:13). Since women usually have loud voices, they are to be easily checked and blamed. Therefore, as far as possible, speaking in tongues should be restrained in the church. Paul teaches from Isaiah 28:11–12, "Thus tongues are a sign not for believers but for unbelievers, while prophecy is a sign not for unbelievers but for believers" (1 Cor 14:22).[68] Some people have gone so far as to say that tongues is a sign of God's curse upon the unbelieving nations as well as a gift of God given to all the nations.[69]

Then how should we understand tongues? Paul also asked, "What, then, brothers? When you come together, each one has a hymn, a lesson, a revelation, a tongue, or an interpretation. Let all things be done for building up" (v. 26). Whatever you do, do it for the building up of the church. This is a foundational rule for using the gifts of God, and it is particularly true for speaking in tongues. Paul does not prohibit speaking in tongues in the church, but he commands its use to be restrained for the purpose of building up.

Fifth, let there be an interpreter. Paul says further, "If any speak in a tongue, let there be only two or at most three, and each in turn, and let someone interpret. But if there is no one to interpret, let each of them keep silent in church and speak to himself and to God" (vv. 27–28). There must be an order and an interpreter in the case of speaking in tongues in the church. If not, the

---

68. This verse is a prophetic promise of the Lord to the Ephramites, who had not obeyed his word, that he would pour out the prepared curses by sending the word through the Gentiles. Therefore, the "tongue" mentioned here is an ordinary "different language," not an unintelligible voice spit out from an ecstatic condition.

69. Among the people who assert this are MacArthur, *Charismatic Chaos*, 227–32; and Robertson, "Tongues," 53 and *Final Word*, 41–51.

The Related Themes and Their Applications

believer should speak to himself and God. Paul asks a question about speaking in tongues and then answers himself: "For if I pray in a tongue, my spirit prays but my mind is unfruitful. What am I to do? I will pray with my spirit, but I will pray with my mind also; I will sing praise with my spirit, but I will sing with my mind also" (vv. 14–15). He does not nullify tongues, but he thinks it is an imperfect way to pray. In 1 Cor 13:8, 10 he says, "When the perfect comes, the partial will pass away. The tongues will cease."

Paul says that he will pray and sing with his spirit as well as with his mind. This does not mean that he will separate his spirit from his mind. Rather, he wants to pray and sing with his spirit and mind united together. The meaning of praying with the mind is to pray with an ordinary, normal, and understandable language. When we pray in a normal language, the prayer will be with the Spirit.

Prophecy

The Meaning of Prophecy

The word "prophecy" used in the Bible needs more accurate definition than any other term for believers. Prophecy is not to foretell the something that will take place in the future. It is not a diviner's job to tell the destiny of man or the world to come. A biblical prophecy is to speak for God and a prophet is a spokesman of God. God chooses his prophet freely and gives his word to speak for him to his people. We call this "to prophesy." God uses language for this communication. However, for a certain cases God uses a prophetic action besides language to deliver his will. Therefore, the Hebrew word *nābā'* does not always means to communicate with languages.

Samuel, after he anointed Saul to be the king of Israel, giving the sign for the Lord's anointment, told him to meet a group of prophets coming down from the high place with various kind of musical instruments prophesying (1 Sam 10:5). We don't know exactly what and how did they prophesied, but Saul could see that

Samuel was right and the Lord had anointed him to be a king. The prophets did not speak any words to Saul, but their actions were showing the meaningful messages of the Lord to him. In a similar case, Saul sent his messenger to take David to kill him, but they saw the company of prophets prophesying (*nebî'îm*) and Samuel was standing as head over them, the Spirit came over them, and they also prophesied (*wayyiṯnabbe'ū*). And Saul himself went to Samuel and he stripped off his clothes before him and he too prophesied (*wayyiṯnabbē*, 1Sam 19:21–24). Saul and his messengers obviously did not play the role of spokesmen of God at this point, but it is said, "Is Saul also among the prophets?" Though this seems to be a saying of mockery about him, they were prophesying something by their action. They were delivering a message of God not by their lips but by their action to the people as well as to Saul himself. God was revealing by his Spirit to them that Saul's effort to take David was not the will of God.

This kind of prophetic action can be seen more clearly in the case of Isaiah, Jeremiah, Ezekiel, and Hosea etc. Isaiah lost the sackcloth for his waist and walked naked and barefoot for three years (Isa 20:2–3). Jeremiah bought the field of Hanamel, his cousin, as the rumor of war was spreading (Jer 32:8). Ezekiel buried the dead body of his wife without any funeral ceremony according to the word of God (Ezek 24:15–24). These kinds of unusual behaviors of prophets were the prophetic actions which signified and symbolized the coming destruction of Judah and the tragic fate of the inhabitants of Jerusalem. The prophets were to deliver the message of God not only by their lips but also with their actions. In Num 11:24–30, God called the seventy elders of Israel to the tent of meeting in order to appoint them to aid Moses. He took some of the Spirit that was on Moses and put it on them. As soon as the Spirit was on them they prophesied (*wayyiṯnabbe'ū*).

Accordingly, from the above examples we can see that the word *nābā'* is used for delivering the message of God not only by the lips of prophets, but also by their symbolic actions. Prophecy is a comprehensive activity of the servant or messenger of God,

The Related Themes and Their Applications

delivering the word of God as well teaching and explaining it, i.e., interpreting it.

In the New Testament, however, the office of prophet is widely open to all believers. The hope of Moses (Num 11:9) and the prophecy of Joel (2:28–29) were fulfilled by the baptism of the Holy Spirit. The Great Commission that Jesus gave to disciples to baptize all the nations and to teach them to observe his commandments was about making them into new covenant prophets. By baptism all believers are brought in union with Christ in his death and resurrection and become members of his body through the work of the Holy Spirit. Therefore, all believers are baptized by the Holy Spirit at the time of water baptism and simultaneously all believers become the new covenant prophets. Gaffin writes rightly on this point:

> We should recognize first of all that according to the New Testament all believers are prophets; the whole church is a congregation of prophets. Analogous to the Reformation insistence on the universal priesthood of believers, we may speak of the "prophethood" of all within the new covenant community, in the sense that words of God (cf. Rom 3:2) are accessible to all, and that by the Spirit's work the law and statues of the covenant are testimony written in the hearts and manifested in the lives of all (cf., e.g., Isa 59:21; Jer 31:33; Ezek 36:27; 2 Cor 3:3ff; 1 John 2:27).[70]

However, he attests that the gift of prophecy was given only to some, not all, in the church and it is revelatory gift, that is, it brings to the church the word of God in the primary and original sense. This means that the gift of prophecy was given only to the apostles and some of disciples who wrote the Bible, and it has been ceased after the apostles.[71]

At this point we are to remember the process of how the prophet came to be known as the mouth of God and his proclamation was recognized as the words from God among the covenant

---

70. Gaffin, *Perspectives*, 59. Barrett, *Acts*, 527–31.
71. Gaffin, *Perspectives*, 59, 89–102.

community of Israel. Evidences and signs were required for the prophets in order to serve his people as the men of God (*'îš haĕlōhîm*). Even Moses and Jesus himself were recognized as the prophets of God by the word they delivered and testified by God through their supernatural deeds in order to accomplish their prophetic mission. But in New Testament the believers are called to be prophets by the baptism of the Holy Spirit and all believers can prophesy, but the canonical and revelatory prophecy was screened and recognized as such by the people and testified by God himself. God gave his words to his servants and had some of the words be recorded to be remained as the canonical books. He did not set any standard to distinguish between canonical prophets and non-canonical prophets. The Holy Spirit came upon the disciples at the same time and at the place to prophesy. All the disciples were granted the same gifts of prophecy. However, canonical prophecy ceased because the canonical prophecy said so (Heb 1:2; Rev 22:18–19).

Prophecy as the Gifts

The Bible teaches that prophecy is also a kind of gift from God like tongues. Paul begins his teaching on the gifts in 1 Cor 12 by saying, "Now concerning spiritual gifts, brothers, I do not want you to be informed." And he mentions existence of various gifts in verse 4 and in verses 8–10 he lists various kinds of gifts including prophecy (v. 10). In 14:26 Paul asks his audience, "What then, brothers? When you come together, each one has hymn, a lesson, a revelation (ἀποκάλυψις), a tongue, or an interpretation. Let all things be done for building up." Paul here does not use "a revelation" instead of prophecy. He is saying that there is a revelation in the church. What, then, is the difference between a revelation and prophecy? The literal meaning of "revelation" is an action uncovering, disclosing, or revealing the divine plan, purpose, or action. Thus, the revelation of God is to reveal himself to man. Man cannot know the invisible God by himself. Only when God reveals himself man know him. God has shown to man his invisible attributes, namely, his eternal power and divine nature since the creation of the world (Rom 1:20). God has revealed through his creatures his existence, his power, and his character so that we can know God when we see his creatures. However, this general revelation is not enough for us to know our sinfulness and the way of salvation from it. Thus, God revealed himself specially to his appointed prophets and let them speak for him. The prophets in the Bible delivered the message of God directly to the people and wrote it in the Bible. This special revelation was completed by the prophets and the apostles. Now there is no more special revelation, because God and God's way of salvation have been completely written in the Bible (Heb 1:1–2). The general revelation is not enough for us to know the way of God's salvation.

At this point, the question is whether God is still giving a new revelation to his people besides those prophets, i.e., the existence of new revelation for the salvation of sinners. If there is still revelation, there is also still prophecy now. Many of the traditional churches teach that since the apostles' role as prophets has ceased, there are no more revelations, prophecies, and tongues. However, Paul clearly teaches here the existence of prophecy. Since there is revelation in the church, there is also prophecy. Now we need to distinguish between the prophecy as a biblical revelation and prophecy as a gift to interpret the messages of God in the Bible and teach them to the church. Paul is teaching here that God gave a gift of prophecy, a prophetic activity to a certain people in the church to interpret and teach the biblical revelation.

Prophecy and Tongues

Paul exhorts the Corinthians, "Now I want you all to speak in tongues, but even more to prophesy" (1 Cor 14:5). After crossing the Red Sea in the wilderness, Moses expressed his desire to Joshua that the Spirit would come upon all the people of the Lord and cause them to prophesy as did the seventy elders (Num 11:25–35). A prophet is a spokesman of God. Prophesying is used to teach the word of God. Accordingly, the one who prophesies speaks to people for their edification, encouragement, and consolation (*oikodomēn kai paraklēsin kai paramythian*, 1 Cor 14:3). Believers should earnestly desire spiritual gifts, especially prophecy (v. 1). The one who speaks in a tongue speaks not to men but to God, and no one understands him because he utters mysteries in the Spirit. Thus, Paul defines his position on this issue: "Nevertheless, in church I would rather speak five words with my mind in order to instruct others, than a thousand words in a tongue" (v. 19). He further goes on to say, "But if all prophesy, and an unbeliever or outsider enters, he is convicted by all, he is called to account by all, the secrets of his heart are disclosed, and so, falling on his face, he will worship God and declare that God is really among you."

Ultimately, prophecy is for building up the church. The disciples of Christ, particularly those who are called and ordained to be the prophets of the new covenant by the baptism of the Holy Spirit, should seek to prophesy rather than to speak in tongues. The meaning of prophesying here is not to predict the future destiny of man or of the world, but to proclaim the word of God written in the Bible, interpret it, and teach how to apply it in contemporary life. The prophet speaks on God's behalf what God wants to speak to his people. Believers, as prophets, should actively play the role of God's mouthpiece. However, there should be a rule of prophesying in the church.

First, we should acknowledge that there is revelation in the church. Paul says, "When you assemble, each one has a psalm, has a teaching, has a revelation, has a tongue, has an interpretation" (1 Cor 14:26). This saying of Paul clearly acknowledges the existence of revelation among the Corinthian believers. Since there is a revelation, there is prophecy. However, some people say that there is no longer any revelation and that it stopped with the cessation of the apostles' activities. As a reason for the cessation of prophecy today, they quote Hebrews 1:1–2:

> Long ago, at many times and in many ways, God spoke to our fathers by the prophets, but in these last days he has spoken to us by his Son, whom he appointed the heir of all things, through whom also he created the world.

The Related Themes and Their Applications

According to cessationists, Jesus, the Son of God, came to this world as prophesied in the Old Testament and revealed himself to us in the last days. The prophecy was fulfilled by Jesus and there is no more revelation. Therefore, they assert that there is only the illumination of the Holy Spirit and no revelatory activity today. However, the illumination of the Holy Spirit is a revelatory activity that makes known the mystery of God's salvation in the Bible, which is God's special revelation.[72] Therefore, we are to begin with the presupposition that since there is revelation, there is prophecy. God is omniscient, omnipotent, and omnipresent. God can do whatever he wants. Salvific revelation through Christ has already been accomplished and is finished, but God still reveals himself to us in various ways.

Second, Paul admonishes, "Let two or three prophets speak, and let the others weigh what is said" (1 Cor 14:29). Collective and simultaneous prophesying is also prohibited as in the case of tongues. If a revelation is made to another person, the first should be silent (1 Cor 14:30) in order that all may prophesy one by one, learn, and be encouraged (v. 31). Revelation here means something divinely spoken in an audible language to be presented and explained. But we cannot say that all prophecies come from God and that all things are edifying and useful for building up the church, because Satan can also use a man as his agent to prophesy. Thus, Paul says, "Let others weigh what is said" (v. 29). The word "*diakrinō*" (διακρίνω) means "to judge" or "evaluate carefully." In the Old Testament, the words proclaimed by the prophets were judged and evaluated as to whether they came from God or

---

[72] Calvin, *Institutes*, I.7.4; I.9.3. WCF, I.5–6. Grudem differentiates between the function of apostolic teaching and congregational prophecy. He states that the cessationalistic view depends on the supposition that the function of prophecy was to provide the church with divinely authoritative guidance until such guidance could be derived from a collection of apostolic writings. However, the function of congregational prophecy was often to provide very special localized information which was needed for the edification of the church and which could only be acquired through a revelation from the Holy Spirit. Access to the major doctrinal teachings contained in the apostolic writings would not make this sort of prophecy obsolete or useless. Grudem, *Gift of Prophecy*, 245.

not (Deut 13:1–5; 18:15–22). The Corinthians were to evaluate whether a man prophesied in accordance with the Bible or not, even though he may have asserted that his prophecy came from God (1 Cor 13:8–10). We have to acknowledge that prophecy will cease and pass away as 1 Cor 13:8 teaches: "Love never ends. As for prophecies, they will pass away; as for tongues, they will cease; as for knowledge, it will pass away."[73] Only the word of God is living and will remain forever. "All flesh is like grass and all its glory like the flowers of the field. The grass withers, and the flower fails, but the word of the Lord remains forever. And this word is the good news that was preached to you" (1 Pet 1:24–25; Isa 40:6–8). Thus, all prophecy must be examined and evaluated in view of the word of God and by the standard of Jesus, the perfect Christ. The prophecy of man is limited by its partiality and temporality. The spirit of the prophet should be checked by other prophesying prophets.

Third, there must be an order in prophesying, just as there is an order in tongues, to promote peace. Paul says that God is not a God of confusion but of peace (1 Cor 14:33). If prophecies bring about confusion in the church, they are not true prophecy. Also, prophecy should build up the church. A so-called prophecy could be heretical and bring about serious conflicts in the church. Therefore, the prophet should always have a heart to fear God, and his prophecy should always seek the benefit, growth, edification, maturity and purity of the church. Since we believers are all his prophets, we are to be required to evaluate our own prophetic experience, behavior, interpretation of the Scriptures and its application according to what Christ and the apostles had taught us.[74] Paul, as he finishes the teaching on prophecy, admonishes believers, the new covenant prophets who were baptized by the Holy Spirit: "So my brothers, earnestly desire to prophesy, and do not forbid speaking in tongues. But all things should be done decently and in order" (1 Cor 14:39–40).

---

73. Grudem, *Gift of Prophecy*, 64.
74. Garland, *1 Corinthians*, 664.

Conclusion

This author has examined a literal translation of Acts 2:3 and proposed that the baptism of the Holy Spirit at Pentecost served as the installation of the new covenant prophets on the basis of a comparison with the Old Testament call narrative. The baptism of the Holy Spirit, the installation ceremony of new covenant prophets, was conducted by the Great Prophet, the risen Christ Jesus, in order to restore the world by the word of God.

The ultimate goal of the eschatological vision of God's restoration is to fill the world with knowledge of God as the waters cover the sea (Isa 11:9). At that time all kinds of creatures will abandon their natural hostilities and live together, and then peace will be established on earth (Isa 2:1–4; 11:6–9; Jer 31:31–34; Ezek 47). For this purpose, God called his prophets and used them as his mouth by putting his words on their mouths to proclaim, interpret, and teach his people how to apply it. Eventually, as the time was fulfilled, God, the word himself, became flesh and came to this world as the prophet to teach the word of God and bring up his disciples as the new covenant prophets. The divine acknowledgement of a prophet, the baptism of the Holy Spirit, was necessary for this ministry of the word for the disciples, as for the prophets of the Old Testament.

In view of this interpretation, the baptism of the Holy Spirit is a once-for-all event in redemptive history and has nothing to do with regeneration and sanctification. Moreover, it is not the beginning of a new covenant or church, nor an epoch-making event in the history of redemption. Those who become disciples after Pentecost officially become Christians at the time of baptism by water when they receive their appointment to be prophets of the new covenant, which is acknowledged by the baptism of the Holy Spirit.

This proposal will bring many benefits in the areas of theology as well as its practice. First of all, the new interpretation of Acts 2:3 will solve conflicts defining the nature of the baptism of the Holy Spirit. There will be no need of long and articulated explanations on the basis of personal and subjective experiences. It is the ceremony of installing believers to be the new covenant prophets for the prophetic ministry of the word. Therefore, those controversial themes such as regeneration, the beginning of the church and covenant, the once-for-allness of the baptism of the Holy Spirit at Pentecost, the fullness of the Holy Spirit, tongues and prophecies, etc. are to be re-examined and explained.

As a practical issue, the importance of water baptism as the baptism of the Holy Spirit should be reconsidered. At the time of the baptismal ceremony, the minister should teach or remind the believers that the baptism of water is the visible symbol of the baptism of the Holy Spirit, the actual sealing of God by his Spirit for his new covenant prophets, and that the believers are given the prophetic office by God in the ceremony. The one being baptized, then, is supposed to be a person that has been united with the Christ in his death and resurrection and has been given the office of prophet to proclaim the word of God in his lifetime on earth. The Protestant church has taught the three offices of Christ and the believers. In particular, they have emphasized the priesthood of all believers. However, they have comparatively emphasized less the prophethood of all believers and have not related the office with baptism. It is time to recognize the role and duty of believers as the prophets of God, the mouths of the Lord.

Bibliography

Atkinson, William P. *Baptism in the Spirit: Luke-Acts and the Dunn Debate.* Eugene, OR: Pickwick, 2011.

Barrett, C. K. *A Critical and Exegetical Commentary on the Acts of Apostles.* 2 vols. Edinburgh: T. & T. Clark, 2004.

Bavinck, Herman. *Magnalia Dei : Onderwijzing in de christelijke Religie naar gereformeerde Belijdenis.* N: Nabu, 2010.

Beale, G. K. *A New Testament Theology: The Unfolding of the Old Testament in the New.* Grand Rapids: Baker, 2011.

Beasley-Murray, George R. *John.* WBC 36. Waco, TX: Word, 1987.

Bergen, Robert D. *1, 2 Samuel.* NAC 7. Nashville: B. & H., 1996.

Bloomberg, Craig L. *Matthew.* NAC 22. Nashville: B. & H., 1992.

Bock, Darrell L. *Luke 9:51—24:53.* BECNT. Grand Rapids: Baker, 1996.

Borchert, G. L. *John 12-21.* NAC 25b. Nashville: B. & H., 2002.

Brown, Raymond E. *The Gospel According to John XIII-XXI.* AB. Garden City, NY: Doubleday, 1970.

Brownson, James V. *The Promise of Baptism: An Introduction to Baptism in Scripture and the Reformed Tradition.* Grand Rapids: Eerdmans, 2007.

Calvin, John. *Commentary on the Book of Psalms.* Translated by James Anderson. Bellingham, WA: Logos Bible Software, 2010.

———. *Commentary on the Book of the Prophet Isaiah.* Translated by William Pringle. Bellingham, WA: Logos Bible Software, 2010.

———. *Commentary upon the Acts of the Apostles.* Translated by Christopher Fetherstone, edited by Henry Beveridge. Bellingham, WA: Logos Bible Software, 2010.

———. *Institutes of the Christian Religion I.* Edited by John R. McNeill, translated by Ford Lewis Battles. Philadelphia: Westminster, 1960.

Carson, D. A. *Showing the Spirit: Theological Exposition of 1 Corinthians 12-14.* Grand Rapids: Baker, 1987.

Chantry, Walter J. *Signs of Apostles: Observation on the Pentecostalism Old and New.* Edinburgh: Banner of Truth Trust, 1978. cited in C. M. Robeck, ISBE 4, 872.

Bibliography

Cole, Graham A. *He Who Gives Life: The Doctrine of the Holy Spirit.* Wheaton, IL: Crossway, 2007.
Cole, R. Dennis, *Numbers.* NAC 38. Nashville: B. & H., 2000.
Cooper, L. Eugene, *Ezekiel.* NAC 17. Nashville: B. & H., 1994.
Craigie, Peter C., Paige H. Kelly, and Joel F. Drinkard Jr. *Jeremiah 1–25.* WBC 26. Grand Rapids: Zondervan, 2016.
Cranfield, C. E. B. *A Critical and Exegetical Commentary on the Epistle to the Romans.* 2 vols. International Critical Commentary. Edinburgh: T. & T. Clark, 1975.
Dahood, M. S. J. *Psalm 1:1–50.* AB. Garden City, NY: Doubleday, 1965.
Danker, Frederick William. *The Concise Greek-English Lexicon of the New Testament.* Chicago: University of Chicago Press, 2009.
Deasley, Alex. "Entire Sanctification and Baptism with the Holy Spirit: Perspectives on the Biblical View of the Relationship." *WTJ* 14 (Spring 1979) 1.
Deere, Jack. *Surprised by the Power of the Spirit : Discovering How God Speaks and Heals Today.* Grand Rapids: Zondervan, 1993.
Dodd, C. H. *A Critical and Exegetical Commentary on the Acts of the Apostles.* Vol. 1. Edinburgh: T. & T. Clark, 2004.
Dunn, James D. G. *Baptism of the Holy Spirit.* Philadelphia: Westminster, 1970.
Dunning, H. Ray. "A Wesleyan Perspective on Spirit Baptism." In *Perspectives on Spirit Baptism: Five Views*, edited by Chad Owen Brand, 181–239. Nashville: B. & H., 2004.
Elwell, Walter A. *Evangelical Commentary on the Bible.* Vol. 3. Grand Rapids: Baker, 1995. ECB. Logos 4.
Enns, Peter. *Exodus.* NIV Application Commentary. Grand Rapids: Zondervan, 2000.
Evans, Craig A. *Mark 8:27—16:20.* WBC 34B. Dallas: Word, 2001.
Fee, Gordon D. *The First Epistle to the Corinthians.* NICNT. Grand Rapids: Eerdmans, 2014.
———. *God's Empowering Presence : The Holy Spirit in the Letters of Paul.* Grand Rapids: Baker Academic, 2011.
Ferguson, Sinclair. *The Holy Spirit.* Contours of Christian Theology. Leicester: InterVarsity, 1996.
———. "John Owen and the Doctrine of the Holy Spirit." The Martin Lloyd Jones Memorial Lecture, 2000. In *John Owen: The Man and His Theology*, edited by Robert W. Oliver, 101–29. Philipsburg: P. & R., 2002.
Frame, John M. *Systematic Theology: An Introduction to Christian Belief.* Philipsburg: P. & R., 2016.
Friberg, Timothy, Barbara Friberg, and Neva F. Miller. *Analytical Lexicon of the Greek New Testament.* Baker's Greek New Testament Library 4. Grand Rapids: Baker, 1981.
Gaffin, Richard B. *Perspectives on Pentecost.* Philipsburg, NJ: P. & R., 1979.
Garland, David E. *1 Corinthians.* BECNT. Grand Rapids: Baker, 2003.
George, A. C. *Dimensions of Spirituality.* Chennel, India: Bethesda, 1997.

Bibliography

Gingrich, F. Wilbur, and Walter Bauer. *A Greek-English Lexicon of the New Testament and Other Early Christian Literature*. 2nd ed. Chicago: University of Chicago Press, 1979.

Goold, William H., editor. *The Works of John Owen*. Edinburgh: 1850-53.

Gresham, John I., Jr. *Charles G. Finney's Doctrine of the Baptism of the Holy Spirit*. Peabody, MA.: Hendrickson, 1989.

Grudem, Wayne. *The Gift of the Prophecy in the New Testament and Today*. Westchester, IL: Crossway:1988.

———. *Systematic Theology: An Introduction to Biblical Doctrine*. Grand Rapids: Zondervan, 1994.

Habel, N. "The Forms and Significance of the Call Narrative." *ZAW* 77 (1965) 292-333.

Hagner, Donald A. *Matthew 1-13*. WBC 33A: Dallas: Word, 1994.

Haroutunian, Joseph, editor. *Calvin: Commentaries*. Library of Christian Classics. Philadelphia: Westminster, 1958.

Hart, Larry. "Spirit Baptism: A Dimensional Charismatic Perspective." In *Perspectives on Spirit Baptism: Five Views*, edited by Chad Owen Brand. Nashville: B. & H., 2004.

Hendriksen, William. *John*. Geneva Series Commentary. London: Banner of Truth Trust, 1954.

Hildebrandt, Wilf. *An Old Testament Theology of the Spirit of God*. Peabody, MA: Hendrickson, 1995.

Horst, F. "Die Visionschilderungen altestamentlichen Propheten." *EvT* 20 (1960) 198.

Horton, Stanley M. "Spirit Baptism: A Pentecostal Perspective." In *Perspectives on Spirit Baptism: Five Views*, edited by Chad Owen Brand, 47-104. Nashville: B. & H., 2004.

Houston, Graham. *Prophecy: A Gift for Today?* Downers Grove, IL: InterVarsity, 1989.

Huey, F. B. *Jeremiah, Lamentations*. NAC 16. Nashville: Broadman, 1993.

Hummel, Charles E. *Fire in the Fireplace: Contemporary Charismatic Renewal*. Downers Grove, IL: InterVarsity, 1978.

Johnson, A. F. *1 Corinthians*. IVP New Testament Commentary 7. Downers Grove, IL: InterVarsity, 2004.

Kaiser, Walter C., Jr. "The Baptism in the Holy Spirit as the Promise of the Father: A Reformed Perspective." In *Perspectives on Spirit Baptism: Five Views*, edited by Chad Owen Brand, 15-46. Nashville: B. & H., 2004.

Keener, Craig S. *Acts: An Exegetical Commentary: Introduction and 1:1—2:47*. Grand Rapids: Baker Academic, 2012.

———. *Gift & Giver: The Holy Spirit*. Grand Rapids: Baker, 2001.

———. *3 Crucial Questions about the Holy Spirit*. Grand Rapids: Baker, 1996.

Kim, Seyoon. *The Origin of Paul's Gospel*. WUNT 2, reihe 4. Tübingen: Mohr, 1981.

Bibliography

Kistemaker, Simon J., and William Hendriksen. *Exposition of the Acts of the Apostles*. Baker's New Testament Commentary 17. Grand Rapids: Baker, 1953-2001.

Knight, George W., III. "The Cessation of the Extraordinary Spiritual Gifts." In *The Beauty and Glory of the Holy Spirit*, edited by Joel Beeke and Joseph A. Pipa Jr., 81-102. Grand Rapids: Reformed Heritage, 2012.

Knowling, R. J. "The Acts of the Apostles." In *The Expositor's Greek Testament*, edited by W. Robertson Nicoll, vol. 2. New York: Doran, n.d.

Lange, J. P., P. Schaff, V. L. Gotthard, C. Gerok, and C. F. Schaeffer. *A Commentary on the Scriptures: Acts*. Belington: Logos Bible Software, 2008.

Lenski, R. C. H. *The Interpretation of the Acts of the Apostles*. Minneapolis: Augusburg, 1961.

Lloyd-Jones, David Martin. *Joy Unspeakable: Power & Renewal in the Holy Spirit*. Edited by Christopher Catherwood. Wheaton, IL: H. Shaw, 2007.

Lyon, Robert W. "Baptism and Spirit Baptism in the New Testament." *Wesleyan Theological Journal* 14/1 (Spring 1979) 14-26.

MacArthur, John F., Jr. *Charismatic Chaos*. Grand Rapids: Zondervan, 1992.

Marguerat, Daniel. "The Work of the Holy Spirit in Luke-Acts: A Western Perspective" In *The Holy Spirit and Church according to the New Testament*, edited by Predrag Dragutinovic, Karl-Wilhelm Niebur, and James Buchanan Wallace. WUNT 354. Tübingen: Mohr Siebeck, 2016.

Marshall, I. Howard. *The Gospel of Luke*. NIGTC. Carlisle: Paternoster, 1978.

Mathews, Kenneth. *Genesis 11:27—50:26*. NAC 1b. Nashville: B. & H., 2005.

Menzies, Robert P. *The Development of Early Christian Pneumatology with Special Reference to Luke-Acts*. JSNTSup 54. Sheffield: JSOT, 1991.

Meyer, H. A. W. *Critical and Exegetical Handbook to the Acts of the Apostles*. Vol. 1. Translated by P. I. Glog, edited by W. P. Dickson. Edinburgh: T. & T. Clark, 1877.

Motyer, J. Alec. *The Prophecy of Isaiah: An Introduction & Commentary*. Downers Grove, IL: InterVarsity, 1993.

Murray, Harris. *The Second Epistle to the Corinthians*. NIGTC. Grand Rapids: Eerdmans, 2005.

Nolland, John. *Luke1:1—9:20*. WBC 35A. Dallas: Word, 2002.

———. *The Gospel of Matthew*. NIGTC. Grand Rapids: Eerdmans, 2005.

Oswalt, John N. *Isaiah*. NIV Application Commentary. Grand Rapids: Zondervan, 2003.

Park, Hyung Yong. *The Holy Spirit and the Church*. Suwon: Hapdong Theological Seminary Press, 2011.

Plastara, James. *The God of Exodus: The Theology of Exodus: Theology of Exodus Narrative*. Milwaukee: Bruce, 1966.

Polhill, John B. *Acts*. NAC 26. Nashville: B. & H., 1992.

Poythress, Vern S. "The Baptism of the Holy Spirit—What Does It Mean?" *Torch and Trumpet* 19/2 (February 1969) 8-10; 19/3 (March 1969) 18-19; 19/4 (April 1969) 7-9.

Bibliography

Reymond, Robert L. *A New Systematic Theology of the Christian Faith*. Nashville: T. Nelson, 1998.

Robertson, O. Palmer. *The Final Word: A Biblical Response to the Case for Tongues and Prophecy Today*. Edinburgh: Banner of Truth Trust, 1993.

———. "Tongues: Sign of Covenantal Curse and Blessing." *WTJ* 38/1 (Fall 1975) 44–54.

Ryken, Leland, James C. Wilhoit, and Tremper Longman III. *Dictionary of Biblical Imagery*. Downers Grove, IL: InterVarsity, 1998.

Sailhamer, John H. *The Pentateuch as Narrative*. Grand Rapids: Zondervan, 1992.

Samarin, William J. *Tongues of Man and Angels*. New York: Macmillan, 1972.

Smith, Gary V. *Isaiah 1–39*. NAC 15A. Nashville: B. & H., 2007.

Sohn, Seock-Tae. *The Divine Election of Israel*. Eugene, OR: Wipf & Stock, 2001.

———. "'I Will Be Your God and You Will Be My People': The Origin and Background of the Covenant Formula." In *Ki Baruch Hu: Ancient Near Eastern, Biblical, and Judaic Studies in Honor of Baruch A. Levine*, edited by R. Chazan, W. W. Hallo, and L. H. Schiffman, 355–72. Winona Lake, IN: Eisenbrauns, 1999.

———. *YHWH, the Husband of Israel: The Metaphor of Marriage between YHWH and Israel*. Eugene, OR: Wipf & Stock, 2002.

Stein, Robert H. *Luke*. NAC 24. Nashville: B&H, 1992.

Stott, John R. W. *Baptism and Fullness*. Downers Grove, IL: InterVarsity,1978.

Thiselton, A. C. *The First Epistle to the Corinthians*. NIGTC. Grand Rapids: Eerdmans, 2000.

Unger, Merrill. *The Baptism and Gifts of the Holy Spirit*. Chicago: Moody, 1974.

———. *New Testament Teaching on Tongues: A Biblical and Historical Survey*. Grand Rapids: Kregel, 1971.

Warfield, Benjamin. *Counterfeit Miracles*. Edinburgh: Banner of Truth Trust, 1918. reprint 1972. cited in C. M. Robeck, Jr. ISBE 4, 872.

Waltke, Bruce K., with Cathi J. Fredricks. *Genesis: A Commentary*. Grand Rapids: Zondervan, 2001.

Watt, J. D. W. *Isaiah 1–33*. WBC 24. Dallas: Word, 1998.

Young, Edward J. *My Servants, the Prophets*. Grand Rapids: Eerdmans, 1952.

Name Index

Aaron, 9, 10
Abel, 77
Abraham, 11, 33, 34
Adam, 11, 32, 57, 61, 77
Alexander, 30
Ananias, 40, 41, 43–45, 68, 82
Annas, 30
Apollos, 46, 47n11, 66, 68
Aquila, 46, 47n11, 66, 68
Athanasius, 74n36
Atkinson, William P., 26n9, 72n32

Barnabas, 45, 46, 49
Barrett, C. K., 23n6, 25n8, 44n9, 47n11, 65n20, 83n53, 99n70
Bavinck, Herman, 78, 78n44
Beale, G. K., 5, 5n6, 6
Beasley-Murray, George R., 58–59, 58n12, 74n36, 75n37, 75n38
Bengel, 58
Bergen, Robert D., 22n5
Betz, 44n7
Bloomberg, Craig L., 16n2
Bock, Darrell L., 19n1
Borchert, G. L., 37n4, 59, 59n15
Brownson, James V., 82n52
Bruce, 58
Bruner, 92n63
Buzi, 13

Cain, 77

Calvin, John, 3, 3n3, 12n5, 21, 22, 22n4, 36n3, 43n6, 58, 65n11, 68n25, 81n51, 86n57, 103n72
Carson, D. A., 93n65
Chantry, Walter J., 93n65
Christ. See Jesus Christ
Cole, Dennis R., 24n7–25n7
Cole, Graham A., 71n31, 74, 74n35
Cornelius, 51, 62–66, 69, 70n28, 72, 91
Craigie, Peter C., 12n5

Daniel, 4, 40
Danker, Frederick William, 8n8
David, 22, 98
Deasley, Alex, 49, 50, 50n14
Deere, Jack, 93n65
Dodd, C.H., 23n6
Dunn, James, xv, 15, 15n1–16n1, 64n18, 72, 76, 76n40, 76n41, 76n42, 78, 80, 80n48
Dunning, H. Ray, 57n10

Eldad, 24
Elijah, 28
Elwell, Walter A., 53n3
Enns, Peter, 11n4
Enosh, 77
Eve, 77
Ezekiel, 4, 12n5, 13, 13n7, 14, 87, 98

Name Index

Fee, Gordon, 93n65
Ferguson, Sinclair, xvi, xvin3, 70n27, 70n28, 71, 71n29, 71n30, 80n49, 86n57
Finney, Charles G., 54
Frame, John M., 77, 77n43
Friberg, Timothy, 8n8, 29n14, 88n60

Gaffin, Richard B., 3, 3n3, 5n6, 29n14, 50, 50n15, 51n16, 99, 99n70, 99n71
Gamaliel, 40
Garland, David E., 81n51, 94n67, 104n74
George, A. C., 93n66
Goold, William H., 86n57
Gresham, John L., 54n7
Grudem, Wayne, 103n72, 104n73

Hagner, Donald A., 16n2, 20n3
Hanamel, 98
Hart, Larry, xv, xvn1, 53n2, 54n6, 72–73, 72n33
Hendriksen, William, 2n2, 49n13
Horst, F., 13n6
Horton, Stanley M., 5n6, 84n55, 84n56, 93n66
Huey, F. B., 12n5
Hull, J. H. E., 59

Isaiah, 4, 12, 13, 21, 22, 36, 37, 41, 44n7, 98

Jacob, 34
James, 28
Jehoshaphat, 46n10
Jeremiah, 11–12, 12n5, 21, 36, 98
Jesus Christ, xvi, 1–2, 5, 15, 15n1, 16, 16n2, 17, 18, 19, 20, 21, 23, 23n6, 25, 27, 28, 29, 30, 31, 32, 35, 36, 37, 39, 40, 41, 43, 44, 47, 47n11, 48, 50, 53, 54, 57, 58, 59, 60, 61, 63, 64, 67, 68, 70, 71, 72, 73, 74, 74n36, 75, 76, 77, 78, 79, 80, 81–82, 83, 84, 87, 91, 92, 94, 99, 100, 103, 104, 105
Joel, 23, 24, 25, 25n8, 99
John (apostle), 27, 30, 36, 38, 39, 42, 58, 59, 60, 61, 84
John the Baptist, 2n2, 16, 21, 26, 28, 29, 38, 53, 63, 67, 70, 81, 87
Johnson, A. F., 81n51
Joses, 28
Joshua, 18n3, 24, 101
Judas, 28

Kaiser, Walter C., xvi, xvin2
Keener, Craig S., 43n6, 47n11
Kim, Seyoon, 44n7
King Saul. *See* Saul (king)
Kish, 45
Kistemaker, Simon J., 2n2, 49n13
Knowling, R. J., 81n51
Koch, 33n1
Kuyper, 55–56, 55n9

Ladd, 57
Lange, J. P., 47n11, 67n23
Lloyd-Jones, David Martin, 54–55, 54n8
Lucius, 46
Luke, xv, 6, 7, 16, 31, 39, 41, 45, 47, 47n11, 48–50, 58, 59, 85
Luther, Martin, 6

MacArthur, John F., Jr., 42n5, 65n21, 69n26, 80, 80n50, 91n62, 92n64, 96n69
Manaen, 46
Marguerat, Daniel, 3n3
Marshall, I. Howard, 29n13, 53n4, 53n5
Mary, 28
Mathews, Kenneth, 34n2
Matthew, 20
Medad, 24
Menzies, Robert P., 26n9
Merrill, 33n1
Meyer, H. A., 6, 6n7

Name Index

Morecraft, 86n58
Moses, 4, 9, 10, 11, 12, 18n3, 24, 27, 34, 98, 99, 100, 101
Motyre, J. Alec, 13n6
Murray, Harris, 26n10

Nicodemus, 72, 74
Noah, 11, 33
Nolland, John, 20n2

Origen, 74n36
Oswalt, John N., 13n6

Pache, 74n35
Packer, 71–72, 71n31
Park, 71n29
Paul, 26, 44n7, 45, 47, 47n11, 48, 49, 51, 66–69, 73, 83, 83n53, 86, 88–97, 100, 101, 102, 103, 104. See also Saul of Tarsus
Peter, 6, 23, 23n6, 24, 25, 25n8, 26, 27, 28, 29, 29n14, 30, 38, 39, 40, 42, 43n6, 51, 62–66, 69, 71, 73, 74, 76, 84, 87–88
Pharaoh, 10
Philip, 41–43, 43n6, 45, 51
Pilate, 70
Plastara, James, 11n4
Polhill, John B., 3n3, 25n8, 68n24
Poythress, Vern S., 27n12, 31
Priscilla, 46, 47n11, 66, 68

Reymond, Robert L., 70n28, 86–87, 87n59

Robeck, 93n65
Robertson, O. Palmer, 92n63, 96n69
Ryon, 53

Samarin, William J., 92n64
Samuel, 45, 97, 98
Sapphira, 40
Saul (king), 24, 45, 97–98
Saul of Tarsus, 41, 43, 44, 44n8, 45, 46, 68, 82–83. See also Paul
Schweizer, 76n40
Seth, 77
Simeon, 28
Simon, 42, 46
Simon Bar-Jonah. See Peter
Sohn, Seock-Tae, 44n8, 78n46
Stauffer, 76n40
Stein, Robert H., 19n1, 80n47
Stephen, 41, 45, 77, 78, 84

Thiselton, A. C., 81n51, 94n67
Thomas, 61
Turner, 58

Unger, Merrill, 16n2, 42n5, 52n1, 65–66, 66n22, 92n63

Warfield, Benjamin, 93n65
Watt, J. D. W., 12n6, 13n6
Westcott, 58

Young, Edward J., 10n3

Scripture Index

OLD TESTAMENT

Genesis
2:7	57, 61
2:10	35
4:26	77
11:7	22
18:17–19	33
20:7	11

Exodus
3:1—4:16	20
3:1–6	11
3:2	3, 6
3:3	4
3:6	11
3:12	13
4:1	27
4:8	28
4:12–13	9
4:15–16	10
6:6	12
7:1–2	10
12:25–27	34
19:18	3

Leviticus
24:2	9n1

24:12	9n2

Numbers
3:16, 17, 51	9
3:16, 39	9
4:37, 41	9
9:15–16	3
9:23	9
11:9	99
11:13–25	18n3
11:24–25	24
11:24–30	24, 98
11:25	18n3
11:25–35	101
11:29	24, 25
22:18	9
23:5	11, 12n5

Deuteronomy
1:26	9
6:12–13, 20–25	34
8:3	9n1
8:6	34
9:12	34
9:23	9
10:16	74

Scripture Index

Deuteronomy *(cont.)*

13:1–5	104
18:15–22	104
18:18	10, 12n5, 15
28:10	44n8
30:3	78n45
30:6	74
33:1	9n1
34:5	9

Judges

2:22	34
6:11–21	20

1 Samuel

3:3–4	4
9:7–8	9n1
10:1	26
10:5	97
16:13	26
19:21–24	98

2 Samuel

23:2	22

1 Kings

1:39	26
12:22	9n1
13:1–34	9n1
13:21, 26	9
14:21, 26, 31	9n1
17:18	9n1
17:24	28
18:38	3
19:11	2n1

2 Kings

1:12, 13	9n1
4:7, 16, 22, 25, 27, 40, 42	9n1
5:8, 14, 15, 20	9n1
6:6, 9	9n1
21:22	34

2 Chronicles

7:14	44n8

Nehemiah

8:7–9	46n10

Psalms

2	16n2
2:28	70
18:21–22	33
36:8	36
46:4	36
147:2	78n45

Proverbs

1:7	34
13:1	34

Isaiah

1–12	20
1:20	9n2
2:1–4	33, 34, 37, 105
2:2–3	34
2:2–5	11
5	5
6	11, 44n7
6:1–13	83n53
6:6–7	12
6:7	9n2, 12n5
11	34, 35
11:1–9	11, 33
11:6–8	34
11:6–9	37, 105
11:9	11, 14, 16n2, 34, 105
11:12	78n45
19:18	22
20:2–3	98
27:13	78n45
28:11–12	96
30	5
31:31–34	33
40:5	9n2
40:6–8	104
44:5	44n8

Scripture Index

49:5	44n7	3:2	87
51:16	11, 12n5	3:14, 22	13, 13n7
56:8	78n45	8:1	13n7
58:6	82	24:15–24	98
58:14	9n2	36:25–26	73
59:21	36, 99	36:26	74
61:1–2	82	36:27	99
62:2	9n2	37:1	13n7
65:17–25	33	37:1–14	57, 61
66:15	2n1	37:9–11	2
		39:18	78n45

Jeremiah

		40:1	13n7
		47	33, 35, 105
1:1–10	11	47:1, 8–9, 12	35
1:4–10	20, 83n53	47:1–12	11, 73
1:9–10	12		
1:19	13		
5:11	9n2	### Daniel	
14:9	44n8	3, 6	40
31:31–34	11, 79, 105	7:9–10	4
31:33	74, 79, 99		### Joel
31:34	37	2:28	23, 24, 25
32:8	98	2:28–29	99
35:5	9n1	3:18	36

Ezekiel

Micah

1	4	4:4	9n2
1–3	11		
1:3	13, 13n7	### Zechariah	
1:27	3	3:2	9n1
2:9—3:2	11	13:1	36
2:29—3:2	12n5	14:8	36
3:1–3	14		

PSEUDEPIGRAPHA (OLD TESTAMENT)

1 Enoch 5

14	5
71	5

Scripture Index

NEW TESTAMENT

Matthew

2:15	16n2
3:16	16n2
11:3	28
16:16	70, 73, 76
16:17	74, 76
21:11, 46	15n1
21:21–27	17
23:27	78
26:28	79
28	20
28:16–20	17, 38
28:18	71
28:18–20	20
28:19	67
28:20	13

Mark

1:8	29
1:38	15
3:15	17
3:31–35	77
3:34–35	73
4:14	37
6:2–3	28
6:15	15n1
7:33, 35	7
8:28	15n1
8:29	70, 73, 76
10:17	29n13
11:28	17
14:65	15n1
15:24	79
16:7	91
16:15	94
16:17	8, 94

Luke

3:10	26, 28–29, 38
3:16	2n2, 3n2, 53
3:22	2, 53, 81
4:14–15	16
4:18–19	82
4:21	82
7:16, 39	15n1
7:16–17	17
9:20	70, 73, 76
10:9–10	18
10:18–19	18
10:25	29n13
16:24	7
17:18–23	28
18:18	29n13
20:1–8	17
22:17	6
22:19–20	79
23:34	6
23:38	70
23:45	80
24:19	15n1
24:31, 32, 45	19
24:32	19
24:45–46	1
24:46–48	20
24:47	1
24:48–49	1
24:49	1

John

1:14	78
3:3	72
3:5	72
3:8	2, 72
3:10	74
4:10	88, 88n60
4:10 (?)	29n14
4:14	36
6:26	26
6:28	29n13
6:68	73
7–8	59
7:37–38	36
7:37–39	74n36

Scripture Index

7:38	74n36	2:7–12	91
7:39	36	2:11	7
12:20	37	2:13	7, 28, 96
12:24	37	2:14–39	23
13:10	73	2:17	24
13:34	79	2:17–18	5
14:16, 26	17	2:17–21	84
14:20, 26	18	2:18	24, 25
14:26	38	2:21	76
14:29	18	2:22–36	25
15:3	73	2:24, 32, 36	71
15:3–4	73	2:32–34	38
15:4	79	2:36	76
15:20	59	2:37	26, 28, 29n13, 69
15:21	60	2:38	29–30, 29n14, 38, 62, 63, 84, 87, 88, 88n60
15:26	38		
16:7	38	2:41	29
17	92	2:42	39, 41, 85, 86
17:8	15	2:45	6
17:18	17	3 and 4	28
17:21	79	3:1–10	30
20:19–20	56	3–4	31, 39
20:22	61	4:4	30
20:27–29	61	4:7	30
21	61	4:8	84
22:19–23	61	4:8–12	30
		4:9	85
Acts		4:13–14	30
1	2	4:29–31	40
1:4–5	1, 54	4:31	84
1:5	1, 3n2, 21, 29, 87	5:1–11	40
1:8	1–2, 38, 71, 86	5:12	40
2	5, 28, 31, 59, 91	5:12–16	40
2:2–4	2	5:20	40
2:3	xvii, 3, 8, 21, 22, 71, 72, 105, 106	5:25, 28	40
		5:42	40
2:3 ESV	3	6:1–17	40
2:3 KJV	3	6:3–4	41
2:3 NAS	3	6:4	41, 85
2:3 NIV	3	6:6	68
2:3 KJV	3	6:7	41, 48, 85, 86
2:4	7, 85	6:8, 10	77, 84
2:6	91	6:10, 55	85
2:7–11	7	7:38	77
		8:1	41

121

Acts *(cont.)*

8:1–3	41
8:14–17	42
8:16	84
9	83n53
9:15–16	44
9:15–20	68
9:17	44
9:18	82
9:20	44
9:31	45, 49
10	91
10:14	84
10:33	62
10:36	76
10:44	64
10:44–45	85
10:44–46	62
10:45	62, 84
10:46	65
10:47	63
10:48	65
11:1	63
11:1–3	65
11:12	85
11:15	64, 64n17, 84
11:16	63
11:17	64, 64n17
11:26	46
12:24	49, 86
13:1	46
13:1–3	86
13:48–49	49
15:35	49
16:30	29n13
17:11	86
18:1–2	66
18:18–21	46
18:25	47n11
18:27–28	47n11
18:29	66
19	91
19:1	67
19:1–2	47n11
19:2	67
19:18–20	47
19:20	49, 86
19:21	48
19:23	49
22:10	29n13
28:23	48, 49, 86
28:30	48
30:31	86

Romans

1:20	101
3:2	99
3:24	88
4:24	70
5:15–16	88
5:17	29n14, 88, 88n60
6	67
6:1–11	82
8:9–10	73
8:26–27	91n62
10:9	76
11:29	88
11:29f	44n7
15:6	22
15:19	27, 31

1 Corinthians

3:16	5n6
6:19	5n6
12	88, 91, 100
12:3	xvi, 73, 76
12:4	100
12:4–6	88
12:7	89
12:8–10	89, 100
12:9, 28, 30, 31	88
12:10	8, 100
12:11	89
12:12	89
12:12–23	90
12:13	71, 80–81
12–14	8, 91
12:18	90
12:25	90

Scripture Index

12:26	90
12:27	89
12:28	90
12:29–30	90
13:1, 8, 14	8
13:1–13	90
13:8	97, 104
13:8–10	104
14:1	90, 102
14:1–5	7
14:2	8, 92
14:3	102
14:4	95
14:5	94, 101
14:6	95
14:9	7, 92
14:11	92, 95
14:12	94, 95
14:14	92
14:14–15	97
14:16	92
14:18	94
14:18–19	93
14:19	102
14:22	96
14:23	96
14:26	94, 94n67, 96, 100, 102
14:27	8, 95
14:27–28	96
14:28	95
14:29	103
14:30	103
14:31	103
14:33	104
14:39	94
14:39–40	104
14:40	95

2 Corinthians

1:11	88
1:21–22	26
3:3ff	99
11:7	88
12:12	27, 31
12:17	94n67

Galatians

1:12,16	94n67
2:2	94n67
2:20	83

Ephesians

2:21–22	5n6
3:7	29n14, 88, 88n60
4:4–6	70n28
5:18	86
5:26	73

Philippians

2:11	8

Colossians

3:16	86

2 Timothy

1:14	86
4:14	88

Titus

3:5	73

Hebrews

1:1–2	101, 102
1:2	100
2:4	27, 31
9:24–26	16n2

James

1.26	7

1 Peter

1:23	37, 73
1:24–25	104
4:10	88

Scripture Index

2 Peter
3–7	32

1 John
2:27	99

Revelation
5:9	8
16:10	7
22:1–5	35
22:18–19	100

WESTMINSTER

Westminster Confession of Faith
1.5, 6 10	86n58
8.8	86n58
10.1	86n58
14.1	86n58
27.3	86n58
I.5–6	103

Westminster Larger Catechism
q. 2	86
q. 2, 4, 43, 67, 72, 76, 155	86n58

Westminster Shorter Catechism
q. 24	86n58

www.ingramcontent.com/pod-product-compliance
Lightning Source LLC
Chambersburg PA
CBHW071441160426
43195CB00013B/1998